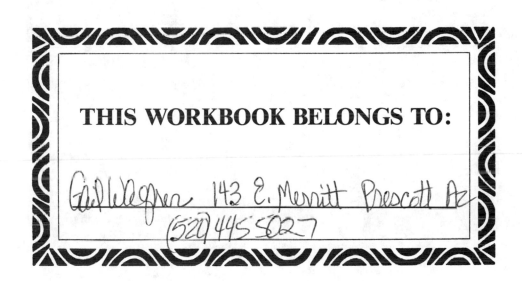

THIS WORKBOOK BELONGS TO:

Gail Wellgren 143 E. Merritt Prescott Az
(520) 445 5027

STEPS TO HEALTHY TOUCHING

A Treatment Workbook for Kids Who Have Problems
with Sexually Inappropriate Behavior

Kee MacFarlane, M.S.W.
and
Carolyn Cunningham, Ph.D.

These materials are designed for children, ages five through
twelve, who exhibit sexually abusive behavior toward other
children; particularly those abuse-reactive children who,
themselves, have been sexually victimized.

STEPS TO HEALTHY TOUCHING
Copyright © 1990, 1988, Kee MacFarlane
and Carolyn Cunningham — text
Copyright © 1990, 1988, KIDSRIGHTS
— illustration
Published by:
  KIDSRIGHTS®
  10100 Park Cedar Drive
  Charlotte, NC 28210
  800/892-5437   704/541-0100

10 9 8 7 6 5

Fifth Printing

Design and illustration by Bob Mortenson
Printed in the United States of America
ISBN: 1-55864-003-7

ACKNOWLEDGMENTS

We would like to thank those who reviewed this workbook and provided encouragement and suggestions for its improvement. They include: Jonathan Ross, Jessica Card, Lynn Sanford, Toni Johnson, Sandra Baker, and Gail Ryan.

We also want to acknowledge the contributions of Al Howenstein, Director of the California Office of Criminal Justice Planning, and Chiquita Sipos, Consultant to the California Youth Authority, for their commitment to, and public funding of, the SPARK program, one of the first treatment programs for pre-adolescent sexual offenders in the country. Recognition also is due the William Simon Foundation, the McKesson Foundation and the Ralph M. Parsons Foundation for their willingness to add private sector support and funding for research and therapies for this very disturbing problem. The development of this workbook was supported in part by grant funds from the William Simon Foundation.

Programs such as: Support Program for Abuse-Reactive Kids (SPARK) at Children's Institute International in Los Angeles; The Young Offenders Program at Glendale Family Services in Glendale, California; Redirecting Sexual Aggression, Inc., in Denver; the Juvenile Victim/Offender Program of the Sacramento Child Sexual Abuse Treatment Program; Center for Child Protection at Children's Hospital in San Diego; and the Child Sexual Perpetrator Network of the C. Henry Kempe National Center in Denver all of which are working to develop models of intervention which are appropriate and effective in treating this age group. Their efforts are helping to create the recognition that minimization and denial of this problem among young children serves no one's interests, and that treatment of child sexual abuse (for victims *and* perpetrators) must begin at the time it is identified. At stake are the futures of these children and their child victims.

DEDICATION

This workbook is dedicated to the first group of children, parents, and therapists in the SPARK program who taught one another about this difficult problem, and who struggled together to find a process for treating it.

These Twelve Steps for Kids and for Parents who live in families where there is a problem with touching have been adapted from The Twelve Steps of Alcoholics Anonymous. The original Twelve Steps have been adapted to apply to many different problems and they have helped many people. We are grateful that Alcoholics Anonymous allows others to use its powerful ideas so that the lives of kids and grownups can become more manageable.

THE TWELVE STEPS
of Alcoholics Anonymous

1. We admitted we were powerless over alcohol — that our lives had become unmanageable.
2. Came to believe that a Power greater than ourselves could restore us to sanity.
3. Made a decision to turn our will and our lives over to the care of God *as we understood Him.*
4. Made a searching and fearless moral inventory of ourselves.
5. Admitted to God, to ourselves, and to another human being the exact nature of our wrongs.
6. Were entirely ready to have God remove all these defects of character.
7. Humbly asked Him to remove our shortcomings.
8. Made a list of all persons we had harmed, and became willing to make amends to them all.
9. Made direct amends to such people wherever possible, except when to do so would injure them or others.
10. Continued to take personal inventory and when we were wrong promptly admitted it.
11. Sought through prayer and meditation to improve our conscious contact with God *as we understood Him,* praying only for knowledge of His will for us and the power to carry that out.
12. Having had a spiritual awakening as the result of these steps, we tried to carry this message to alcoholics, and to practice these principles in all our affairs.

Reprinted for adaptation with the permission of Alcoholics Anonymous World Services, Inc.

CONTENTS

INTRODUCTION FOR GROWNUPS

This workbook has been designed as a therapeutic tool in the treatment of young children, age five through twelve, who have molested or acted out sexually with younger children. Its goals include helping young perpetrators to understand and accept responsibility for their problems, teach them to express their feelings appropriately, and foster the belief that their behavior can be controlled if they learn to monitor warning signals and ask for help when they need it.

The workbook is intended to be a supplement to, not a substitute for, comprehensive treatment of children and families. It can be used in conjunction with either individual or group therapy, although it is recommended for use with small groups consisting of four to eight children of the same sex and close in age. Clinicians are encouraged to conduct parallel parents' groups which meet at the same time. Twelve Steps for Parents of these children have been included in this workbook to help facilitate this parallel process.

BASED ON THE TWELVE STEPS OF A.A.

Based on the Twelve Steps of Alcoholics Anonymous, STEPS TO HEALTHY TOUCHING has been modified to accommodate the younger child's developmental levels and address the problem of child sexual abuse. Reference to God or a Higher Power is included in some of the steps, as it is an important part of most twelve step programs. However, the concept of Higher Power may be interpreted individually, for example, it might symbolize the collective support of the adults in a child's life, or the power of all the children in the world. The concept itself is optional in this workbook, since every step which includes a reference to God is followed by an alternative page which presents the same step without the reference to God.

ABOUT THE STEPS

The steps are presented in the format of a 100 yard football field. The completion of each step is worth an advance of five to twenty yards. Each step includes activities or tasks designed to reinforce the concepts presented. They are designed to be read aloud to children and discussed, prior to completion. The steps also include at least one homework assignment which parents/caretakers are asked to sign before it is submitted. When children complete each step, including homework and a review, they progress five, ten, or twenty yards, depending on the value of that step. When the child finishes all twelve steps, he/she makes a touchdown.

AWARDS

Award certificates are included for presentation at the completion of each step. Therapists are encouraged to make visual progress charts such as individual or group football fields out of poster board or check lists so that children can see the progress they are making. If the football field analogy is felt to be too male-identified or too competitive for a particular treatment population, therapists are encouraged to create their own analogies, such as a staircase to recovery or steps on a rainbow.

USING THIS WORKBOOK

These twelve steps are not intended to constitute a twelve week program. Progress will vary according to the developmental levels of the children, their ability to accept the concepts presented, the nature and extent of their perpetration and victimization, and the number of children in a group. Progress may not always be in a forward direction; children may move back and forth across the field as various issues re-emerge and require further work. Pilot testings of these materials indicate that a time frame for completion of the workbook may by anywhere from fourteen to twenty-eight weeks (based on once-a-week sessions of 1½ to 2 hours, including a snack time).

Therapists are encouraged to utilize their own treatment methods in working through the steps.

There are many additional therapeutic issues, such as children's own sexual victimization, anger management, and sexual identity problems which are not covered in depth in this workbook. Additional activities and homework assignments could be added according to the needs of the children. The words "touching" or "touching problem" are used throughout this workbook to refer to all forms of sexually abusive behavior. Therapists are encouraged to explain to children that this is meant to include all kinds of inappropriate sexual behavior including: exhibitionism, voyeurism, oral copulation, frottage, etc. Periodically it should also be emphasized that not all touching is wrong or hurtful, that there are many forms of acceptable physical contact, and that sexual touching will be acceptable when they are older or grownup, providing that the other person is able and willing to consent to it.

A team approach has proven to be useful in using these materials in a group setting. Placing beans or marbles in a jar or points on a chart to reinforce positive behaviors, and taking them away for negative behaviors, not only lets children see what is expected of them and how they are doing, it exerts the kind of peer pressure which, when controlled, allows them to succeed cooperatively. Group rewards for specified levels of accomplishment might include a special snack, small toys, or a favorite group activity.

Ideally, each child should have his or her own workbook in order to foster a sense of personal investment, possession, and accomplishment. STEPS TO HEALTHY TOUCHING is designed so that most activities can be written or drawn directly onto the pages. If this is not possible, activities should be kept together, in individual folders for each child, so that they can see their own progress and refer back to past statements and expressions of feeling. When children ask to keep particular activities, photocopies should be made for them so that the originals can be preserved in clinical files. Photocopies should also be made of homework assignments so children can take them home. The task of rewriting homework assignments in the original workbook at the beginning of the group session should be considered; it reminds children of their accomplishments and reinforces the concepts introduced during the previous session.

IN CLOSING

Very little literature and few specialized tools are aimed at this unique population of child clients and their families. Although the lessons learned from the treatment of adolescent sexual offenders provide a helpful framework for understanding some of the dynamics of young child perpetrators, the methods and approaches to treatment need to be modified to meet the needs of younger children. Because they generally have less tolerance for didactic presentations or lengthy group/individual discussions, their learning cannot be dependent upon verbal or cognitive skill levels. In addition, an approach which *too* directly focuses on their sexual behavior or victimization is likely to increase their anxiety which, in turn, often leads to acting out, hyperactivity, and disruption of the treatment setting. Therefore, the approach of STEPS TO HEALTHY TOUCHING is one of learning by doing, by analogy, by parallel problem-solving, and by exploring a range of feelings.

Obviously, all approaches to treatment of this population of children must be considered innovative and experimental at this point in time. Clinicians who utilize these materials are encouraged to evaluate their effectiveness and to provide feedback to the authors. We, in turn, would like to acknowledge the contribution of everyone who recognizes the need for early intervention with this population, and is willing to explore new pathways to treatment despite the current lack of guideposts along the way.

TWELVE STEPS FOR PARENTS

1. I acknowledge that my child has been involved in sexually abusive behavior, and that the problem is too big for me or my family to handle alone.

2. I believe that there are people who care about my child and my family who can help us with this problem. (I also believe that a power greater than ourselves can help us if we are open to receiving it.)

3. I have decided to allow people who understand this problem help my family to get control over it.

4. I will stop blaming other people or the "system" for my family's problem and admit how serious this problem has become.

5. I admit to myself, to other people (and to God) exactly what my child has done that is wrong and harmful to others. I also acknowledge the possibility that I may have unknowingly contributed to my child's inappropriate behavior.

6. I am ready to do whatever is necessary to help my child change his/her behavior. I am willing to examine my own behavior, attitudes and feelings so that my family can find better ways to communicate feelings.

7. I am willing to examine my own history of victimization and abusive or addictive behavior so that my own issues will not hinder me from helping my child with his/hers.

8. I recognize that there are things about myself and my family that I can change, and other things that I cannot change. Beginning with my own faults, I am working on changing the things I can.

9. I am learning to recognize the signs and situations where my child may be at risk of further abusive behavior. I am willing to ask for help when I recognize these warning signals.

10. I am ready to acknowledge the harm that my child's behavior has caused, and I am willing to help my child make amends whenever that is possible.

11. I will continue to be aware of my child's problem and I will not respond with impatience or feelings of false security. I recognize that my child needs my help and I will take necessary precautions to help prevent victimization of other children.

12. I will help other parents who have this problem by sharing my feelings and experiences and by helping them to see that they and their children need help.

DISCUSSION GUIDE
FOR THERAPISTS WORKING
WITH PARENTS

The following are suggestions for discussion topics and/or questions to be raised by therapists or group leaders as they work with parents on each of the Twelve Steps for Parents. As with the children's step program, it is anticipated that these discussion topics will take longer than twelve weeks and therapists should consider coordinating them with their children's progress. Parents should be reminded about assisting children with homework assignments which might be shared with parents during the session prior to the due dates. Remember, parents' groups or therapy sessions can be as important as your work with children; the more that parents benefit from the program, the more likely the family is to stay involved.

STEP ONE: Explore parents' feelings about the premise that their child's problem is now the whole family's problem. Do they have feelings of resentment toward their child or anyone else? Do they resent having to come to therapy? Are they ready to admit that the problem is out of control? If not, what would it take? Have they ever had any other problems that were too big to handle alone? What did they do? Who is being responsible for handling this problem?

STEP TWO: Explore parents' concepts of a higher power. This need not include traditional concepts of God, although parents who receive strength from their belief in God might be encouraged to share their feelings. Who are the caring people in the lives of each child and family who might be able to help with this problem? How do people know when someone cares that much? How can parents let them help?

STEP THREE: Discuss with parents whether they feel ready and open to receiving help with

their family's problem. How hard is it to admit the need for help and/or to ask for it? Does it invoke feelings of weakness or failure? Should parents instinctively know how to handle a problem like this? Would they feel differently if the problem were a physical illness? Explore the differences between helping a child gain control over a problem versus being controlling.

STEP FOUR: Ask parents to name the single most likely person or thing to blame for their child's problem. Having aired the feelings associated with that, discuss blaming as a defense mechanism — as a way of putting distance between one's self and the problem. Who has been blamed by others for this problem? Does blaming really help, or does it slow down the healing process? If their children also are victims, can they still be responsible for their actions?

STEP FIVE: Focus on helping parents to let go of their need to minimize their children's behavior. Verbalizing a step-by-step account of exactly what occurred can bring relief associated with fully admitting it to themselves and others. Such admission might also include the possibility that it occurred long before detection, that more happened than is known, and that it could occur again. This also may present the opportunity to explore homophobic feelings regarding children who have been sexual with children of the same sex. Encourage parents to discuss what it is that is wrong with their children's behavior, i.e., the victim's inability to consent due to age; his/her lack of knowledge of consequences; the use of force, trickery, manipulation, or position of power; unseen potential emotional reactions; etc. In keeping with discussions of wrongdoing, emphasize the difference between doing something wrong and being wrong or bad; i.e., the child's behavior was wrong; the child is still a good person.

STEP SIX: Discuss whether there are any ways that the family's dynamics may have contributed to the child's behavior. Are there any negative patterns of communication (such as ways of handling anger, hurt, disappointment, etc.) that children have copied from their parents? Discuss children's needs to feel free to communicate their feelings (both positive and negative), in order to reduce the need to act them out. Explore methods of improving family communication and openness to expressing feelings.

STEP SEVEN: Explore parents' own histories of victimization (physical and/or sexual abuse, battered spouses, exploitation, etc.), as well as prior or present addictive behavior and substance abuse. Discuss the ways that their children's behavior has triggered their feelings or memories of negative events in their own pasts. Examine whether these old issues may be becoming confused with, or feeding into, their children's issues.

STEP EIGHT: Help parents differentiate the things about themselves and their families that can be changed versus those things which cannot be changed. There are many areas to consider: appearance, feelings, behavior, history, attitudes, relationships, circumstances, beliefs, etc. Emphasize that most changes must come from within ourselves — and only if we want to change. What things are parents willing to work to change about themselves that may help with their child's problem?

STEP NINE: What are the warning signs or danger signals in each family that may signify that the child is in emotional trouble? What are the high risk situations to be avoided? What were the circumstances of the original situation(s), and what others might trigger a similar response? What was the emotional climate of the family at the time and/or what emotions was the child expressing? Explore methods or codes whereby children can let parents know if they feel in danger of re-abusing. Help parents develop a plan for what each family will do to help the child regain control during difficult periods. Emphasize that the overconfident belief (by parents or children) that such measures are unnecessary because the problem could never reoccur is, in itself, a danger signal.

STEP TEN: Explore with parents the various ways that their children's victims may have been harmed by their children's behavior. Statements should be personalized (in order to minimize abstraction) by using the names of victims and others involved. Encourage comparisons with victimization experiences of parents and their children in order to promote empathy and reduce defensiveness. Discuss ways in which parents might help children make amends for their behavior. Note: Individual circumstances may indicate that direct amends are *not* advisable. However, symbolic gestures, such as helping a child to write something that is not delivered, or undertaking a restitution project, can substitute for personal contact.

STEP ELEVEN: Discuss parents' natural impatience with the therapeutic process and their desire for this problem to go away. Introduce the idea that, for some people, problems involving inappropriate sexual contact (like those of substance abuse) may be life-long issues which can be *controlled* rather than "cured". Explore the differences between "policing" the activities of children versus being available to help a child and creating an environment which helps provide controls for temptation. Explore the differences between offering trust and helping to build in control factors.

STEP TWELVE: Discuss ways in which the sharing of feelings and experiences has helped parents cope with their problems. Encourage parents to share with each other how they have personally helped one another and/or what they have learned from each other. Explore ways in which they might use this experience, or that of their children, to help parents of children with similar problems.

**From clinician/group leader
to parent/caretaker**

SAMPLE LETTER

Dear Parents or Caretakers,

In order to help with your child's treatment, homework assignments will be given. It would be very helpful if you would review the assignments with your child and encourage him or her to complete the homework before coming to the next therapy session.

In addition, please sign your name on the bottom of each homework assignment after your child completes it.

Thank you for your cooperation and support in this very important aspect of your child's treatment.

Sincerely,

INTRODUCTION FOR KIDS

Everyone usually has one or two big problems that need help. This workbook was made to help you with your problem of touching other kids in ways that are wrong or hurtful. It can also help you with the problem of showing your private parts to kids who don't want to see them. This is a workbook about stuff that most people don't want to talk about: problems with sexual behavior.

TWELVE STEPS

There are 12 steps to follow and learn. You can think of this workbook as kind of a football game that you really need to win. Each step has tasks for you to do, questions for you to answer, and things for you to think about. At the end of every step you will gain yards toward your touchdown. When you're all done with the workbook, you'll have gained 100 yards and scored a touchdown. Some of the steps are worth more yards than others because some are harder than others. Some steps are going to take longer than others to finish, and sometimes you might forget things you learned in a previous step and have to go back and try it again. That's okay, this is not a race. It is a group of steps that can help you to learn about yourself, your feelings, and your problem with touching.

HOMEWORK

Now there *is* one part you might not like — HOMEWORK (Yuck! Homework!). Yes, there is *some* work for you to do at home, but it isn't the kind of hard or boring homework you sometimes get at school. It's more like a bunch of little projects to figure out, and it won't take you very long to do them. But, you will have to get them signed by one of your parents or a grownup that you live with before you hand them in, or you won't be able to go on to the next step. It helps to have some grownups on your team, anyway, because you're going to need some help to beat this touching problem. Every team needs many players and even the best player can't win a football game by himself!

YOUR GOAL

Each time you finish a step you will be working to make your touching problem go down. That's why the goal is to get a touchdown! When you finish the twelfth step you will have reached your goal of learning to control your problem of touching other people in hurtful ways. A true touchdown! It takes a lot of work to control a big problem, but reaching the goal will make you stronger and healthier. Remember, many people are on your team and are cheering for you, so give it your best.

12
STEPS FOR KIDS
who have problems with touching

1. I have a problem with touching that is too tough for me to handle by myself. It is bigger than I am.

2. I believe that there are people who care about me who can help me with my touching problem. I believe that God will help me too, if I ask.

3. I am making up my mind to let people who know and understand this problem help me to get power over it.

4. I have decided to stop blaming other people or events for everything, and admit how big my problem really is.

5. I admit to myself, to other people, and to God, exactly what I have done that is wrong and harmful to others.

6. I am ready to give up my problem (even though sometimes the touching feels good), and find another way to show my feelings.

7. I am learning that there are some things about myself that I can change, and other things that I cannot change. I am working on changing the things I can.

8. I accept that I cannot change other people or their behavior. They are the only ones who can change themselves — and only if they want to. This includes my parents, other grownups, and my friends.

9. I am learning to recognize the times when I need help from others, including God, and I am willing to ask for help because I need it.

10. I have made a list of everyone I have hurt by my behavior (including myself), and I will try to make up, in any way I can, for the harm I have caused.

11. I continue to think about my problem, and I am willing to ask for help if I feel it coming back.

12. I will help other kids who have this problem by sharing my own problem and feelings, and by helping them to see that it is too tough for them to handle by themselves.

12
STEPS FOR KIDS
who have problems with touching

1. I have a problem with touching that is too tough for me to handle by myself. It is bigger than I am.

2. I believe that there are people who care about me who can help me with my touching problem.

3. I am making up my mind to let people who know and understand this problem help me to get power over it.

4. I have decided to stop blaming other people or events for everything, and admit how big my problem really is.

5. I admit to myself and to other people exactly what I have done that is wrong and harmful to others.

6. I am ready to give up my problem (even though sometimes the touching feels good), and find another way to show my feelings.

7. I am learning that there are some things about myself that I can change, and other things I cannot change. I am working on changing the things I can.

8. I accept that I cannot change other people or their behavior. They are the only ones who can change themselves - and only if they want to. This includes my parents, other grownups, and my friends.

9. I am learning to recognize the times when I need help from others, and I am willing to ask for help because I need it.

10. I have made a list of everyone I have hurt by my behavior (including myself), and I will try to make up, in any way I can, for the harm I have caused.

11. I continue to think about my problem, and I am willing to ask for help if I feel it coming back.

12. I will help other kids who have this problem by sharing my own problem and feelings, and by helping them to see that it is too tough for them to handle by themselves.

"I have a problem with touching that is too tough for me to handle by myself. It is bigger than I am."

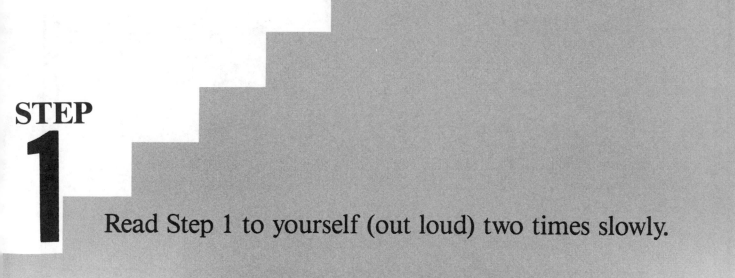

STEP

1

Read Step 1 to yourself (out loud) two times slowly.

FEELINGS
I HAVE WHEN I
ADMIT THAT I HAVE
A PROBLEM

Step One is one of the hardest but most important steps.

Lots of kids feel embarrassed or ashamed or scared inside when they have to talk about their problems with touching. They do all kinds of things to avoid talking about it. They clown around, blame others, change the subject, act really angry or talk non-stop about other subjects. Some people call these things defenses or masks. Some kids use defenses to hide their problems the way a mask hides your face.

How do you *really* feel when you start to admit to yourself that you have a big problem? Draw or write the feelings on this page.

MASKING YOUR FEELINGS

On Halloween we wear real masks to hide our faces. But sometimes we wear "imaginary masks" — the kind that other people can't see. Imaginary masks hide our feelings from other people. You are wearing an imaginary mask when you're pretending to feel something that you don't really feel.

Examples of imaginary masks are:

■ Acting like everything is fine when it isn't
■ Saying you don't care about something when you do
■ Pretending to be super nice when you're really angry inside
■ Acting angry when what you really feel is hurt.

What masks do you wear that keep you from admitting to yourself that you have a problem with touching? On this page or another piece of paper draw the mask or masks that you wear to hide your feelings.

You and your group can make "feelings masks" out of paper plates which you can give to each other to wear when you are acting like you are feeling certain things. For example, clown, grouch, people pleaser, sad sack, or the "who cares kid".

Picture yourself taking off the masks. Draw a picture of yourself without any masks, saying to yourself, "I have a touching problem that is too tough for me to handle by myself. It is bigger than I am."

Draw your problem right next to the picture of you. How much bigger is it than you?

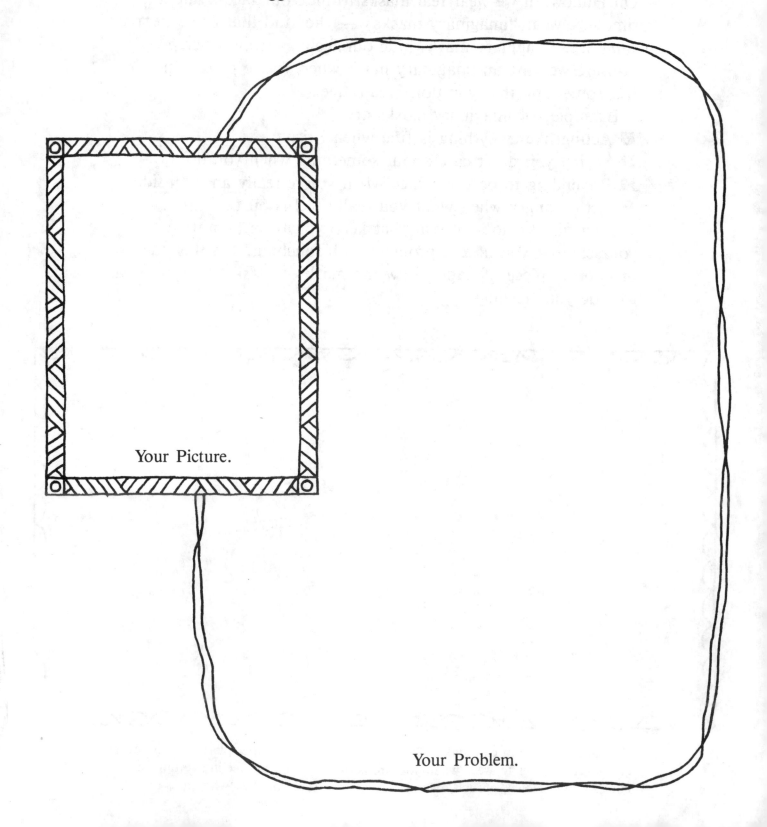

Your Picture.

Your Problem.

STEP 1
HOMEWORK
ASSIGNMENT

Once a day for the next week, remind yourself that you have a problem that is bigger than you are. It will help you to remember if you do it at the same time every day — like while you brush your teeth or take a bath. Just pause for a minute and say to yourself, "I have a touching problem that is too tough for me to handle by myself."

Also, pay attention to any times when you are pretending to feel things that you don't really feel or when you are hiding your real feelings. If you catch yourself putting on an "imaginary mask", stop and think about what you are *really* feeling. Then go and tell someone what it is.

_____   _____

      (Parent Signature)   (Date)

32

The Step that I learned last week said (write down your answer or have someone else write it for you.)

_____

_____

_____

_____

_____

I practiced what I learned last week by _____

_____

_____

_____

_____

_____

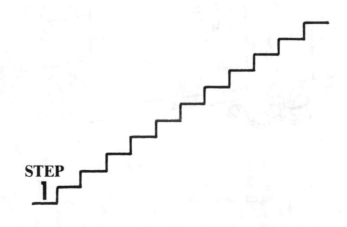

STEP
1

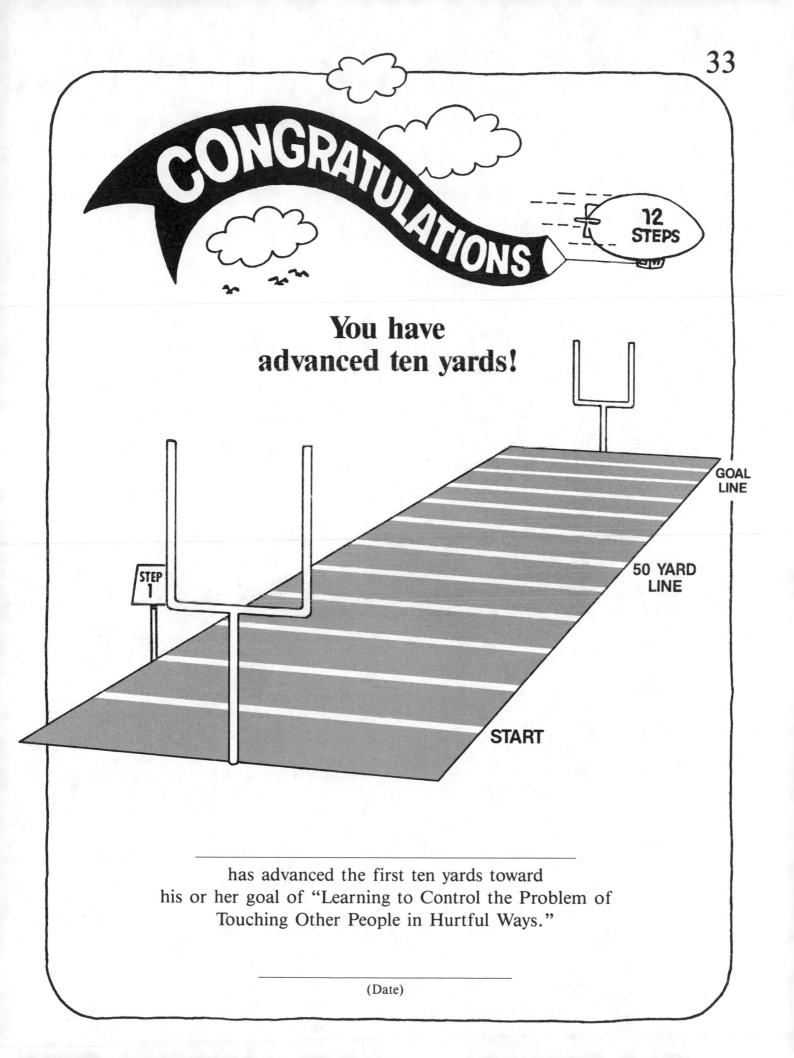

You have advanced ten yards!

has advanced the first ten yards toward
his or her goal of "Learning to Control the Problem of
Touching Other People in Hurtful Ways."

_____

(Date)

"I believe that there are
people who care about me who
can help me with my problem.
I believe that God will help
me too, if I ask."

STEP
2

Read Step 2 to yourself (out loud) two times slowly.

"I believe that there are people who care about me who can help me with my problem."

ALTERNATE STEP

2

Read Step 2 to yourself (out loud) two times slowly.

PEOPLE WHO CARE ABOUT ME

Lots of people care about you. How do you know when people care about you?

Draw a picture or make a list of the special people in your life who care about you. Write their names next to their pictures. Put a check mark next to the people who you will let help you with your problem. Talk about the ways that these special people might be able to help you.

This is _____

This is _____

This is _____

This is _____

This is _____

GOD CARES ABOUT ME

(Optional Exercise)

People have different ideas about what God looks like. Some people don't have any picture of God in their minds, but they do believe that there is a "higher power" that is more powerful than they are. Your "higher power" could even be a person or people that you know. It could be a group you're in, or it could be something less real — like a rainbow or the sky. A "higher power" gives you help and strength...the feeling of caring about you.

Draw a picture of the way you see God or your higher power. Then draw yourself next to your God or higher power and think about the help you are getting. Think about being cared for and protected by your higher power. Guess what? You are!!

STEP 2
HOMEWORK
ASSIGNMENT

Pick one or more of the special people in your life and ask them to help you with something this week. It's better if you ask for help with a feelings problem or something that is bothering you, than with something ordinary like your math homework. Maybe they can help you understand your feelings about something or someone — maybe they once felt that way.

See if it's hard for you to ask for help and how it felt after you did it. Practice doing it whenever you can.

The feeling or problem that I needed help with was: _____

_____

_____

_____

_____

The person who helped me was: _____

_____

_____

_____

_____   _____
(Parent Signature)   (Date)

The Step that I learned last week said (write down your answer or have someone else write it for you.)

_____

_____

_____

_____

_____

I practiced what I learned last week by _____

_____

_____

_____

_____

_____

_____

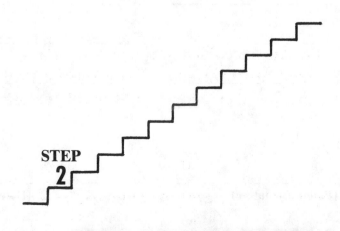

STEP
2

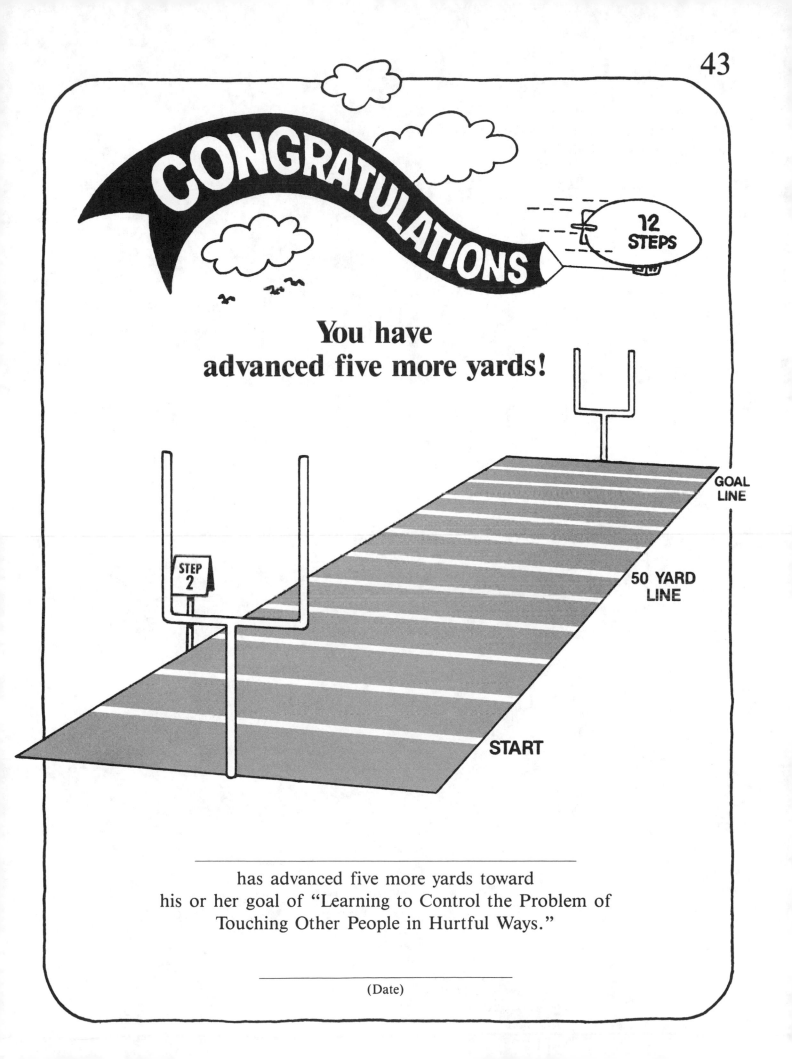

CONGRATULATIONS

12 STEPS

You have
advanced five more yards!

GOAL LINE

50 YARD LINE

STEP 2

START

_____

has advanced five more yards toward
his or her goal of "Learning to Control the Problem of
Touching Other People in Hurtful Ways."

_____
(Date)

"I am making up my mind to let people who know and understand this problem help me to get power over it."

STEP

3

Read Step 3 to yourself (out loud) two times slowly.

ASKING FOR HELP

Some kids feel that it is babyish to need help or ask for help. It's really not babyish at all to ask for help. You are growing up when you begin to learn that there are some things you can do all by yourself and some things or problems for which you need help. People who have problems that are bigger than they are *always* need to ask for help.

Think about the people who know about your problem with touching. Draw a picture that shows them helping you.

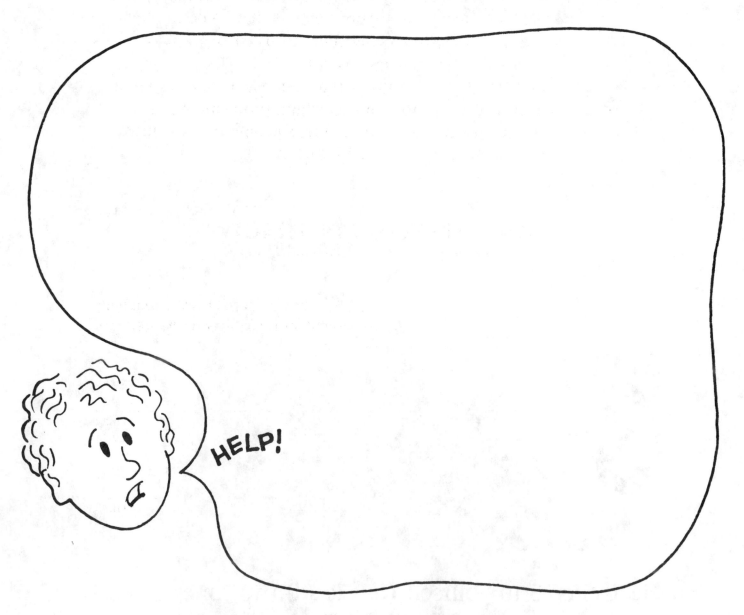

How do you feel about telling someone more about your problem?
How do you feel about letting someone help you with it?

STEP 3
HOMEWORK
ASSIGNMENT

This week, talk to someone about your problem with touching. It can be someone who already knows about it, like one of your parents or another member of your family, but tell them something more than they already know. Don't try to act like your problem is no big deal or as if you already have control over it. Tell them that your problem is too tough for you to handle by yourself and ask for their help. Figure out together some of the ways that they might help (like being there to listen or to help you in case the urge to touch comes back).

Try to find at least three ways that that person, or one way that three people, can help you with your touching problem. Write them down and get either one, two, or three people to sign their initials showing that they agree to help you.

THE HELPING CONTRACT

I recognize that _____ has a problem with touching, and I agree to help him/her to get better control over it in the following way(s):

1 _____

_____   _____
                                             (Initials)

2 _____

_____   _____
                                             (Initials)

3 _____

_____   _____
                                             (Initials)

_____   _____
        (Parent Signature)   (Date)

48

The Step that I learned last week said (write down your answer or have someone else write it for you.)

_____

_____

_____

_____

_____

I practiced what I learned last week by _____

_____

_____

_____

_____

_____

_____

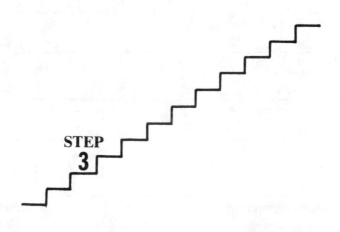

STEP
3

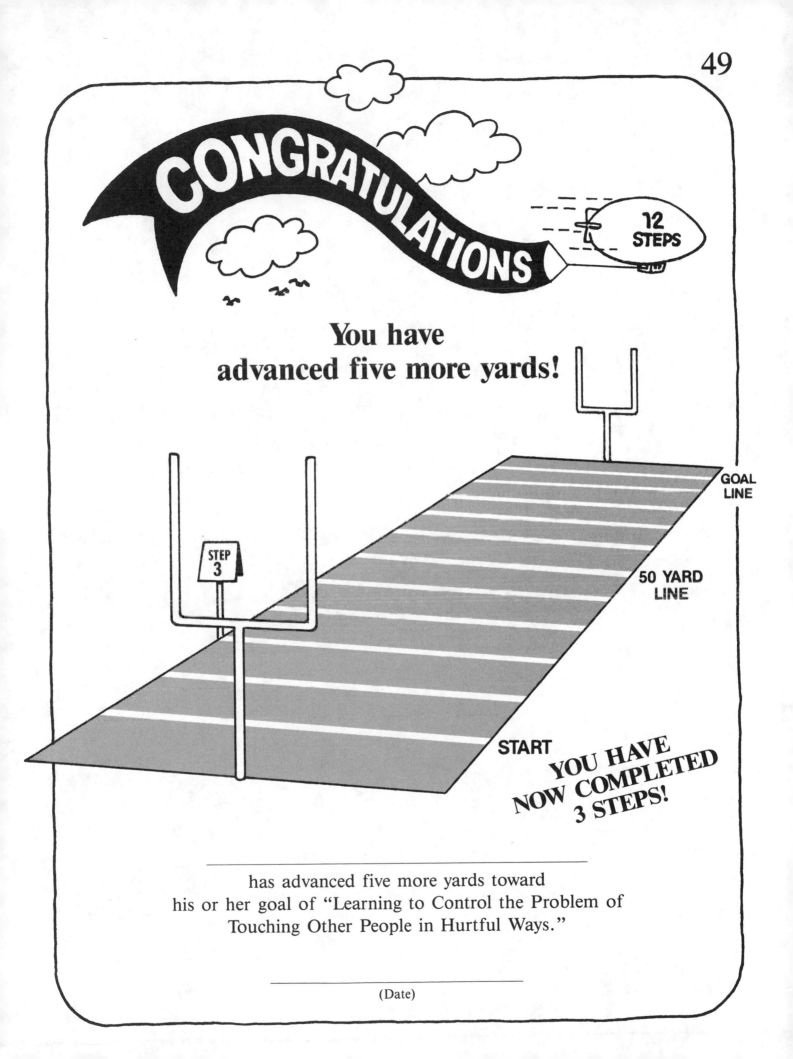

CONGRATULATIONS

12 STEPS

You have advanced five more yards!

GOAL LINE

50 YARD LINE

STEP 3

START

YOU HAVE NOW COMPLETED 3 STEPS!

_____

has advanced five more yards toward
his or her goal of "Learning to Control the Problem of
Touching Other People in Hurtful Ways."

_____

(Date)

"I have decided to stop blaming other people or events for everything, and admit how big my problem really is."

STEP

4

Read Step 4 to yourself (out loud) two times slowly.

ME & MY
BLAMING MASK

Blaming is a mask many people wear when they feel too afraid to face or admit that they have a problem. Some kids blame the person they touched by saying, "He made me do it," or, "She liked it." Some kids blame their parents by saying, "My mom made me mad...that's why I did it." Some kids blame everyone for everything.

Make a picture of you taking off your blaming mask.

MY
BLAMING
LIST

On this page make a list of whom you have blamed for your touching problem, and what part of it you blamed them for causing.

People I have blamed: **What I blamed them for:**

1 _____   1 _____

_____   _____

_____   _____

_____   _____

2 _____   2 _____

_____   _____

_____   _____

_____   _____

3 _____   3 _____

_____   _____

_____   _____

_____   _____

4 _____   4 _____

_____   _____

_____   _____

_____   _____

MY
STOP SIGN

Make a Stop Sign* that says **"Stop & Think!"**
This is a reminder that you must stop blaming other people for your problem with touching. You might want to put your Stop Sign up in your room at home to remind yourself to Stop and Think.

NO MORE BLAMING

I CAN HANDLE IT

FACE UP TO IT

TAKE RESPONSIBILITY

BLAMING STINKS

IT'S LAME TO BLAME

BLAMING IS FOR LOSERS

BLAMING IS KIDS' STUFF

*Cardboard and popsicle sticks work well.

STEP 4
HOMEWORK
ASSIGNMENT

WEEKLY BLAMING LIST

Make a list of the times during the week you caught yourself blaming others for things that you did.

I blamed or started to blame:
(person's name)   **For:**

1 _____   1 _____

_____   _____

_____   _____

2 _____   2 _____

_____   _____

_____   _____

3 _____   3 _____

_____   _____

_____   _____

4 _____   4 _____

_____   _____

_____   _____

_____   _____
(Parent Signature)   (Date)

56

The Step that I learned last week said (write down your answer or have someone else write it for you.)

_____

_____

_____

_____

_____

I practiced what I learned last week by _____

_____

_____

_____

_____

_____

_____

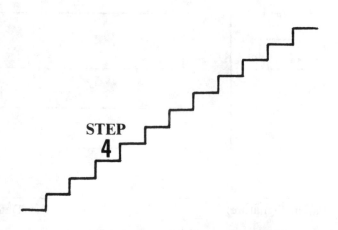

STEP
4

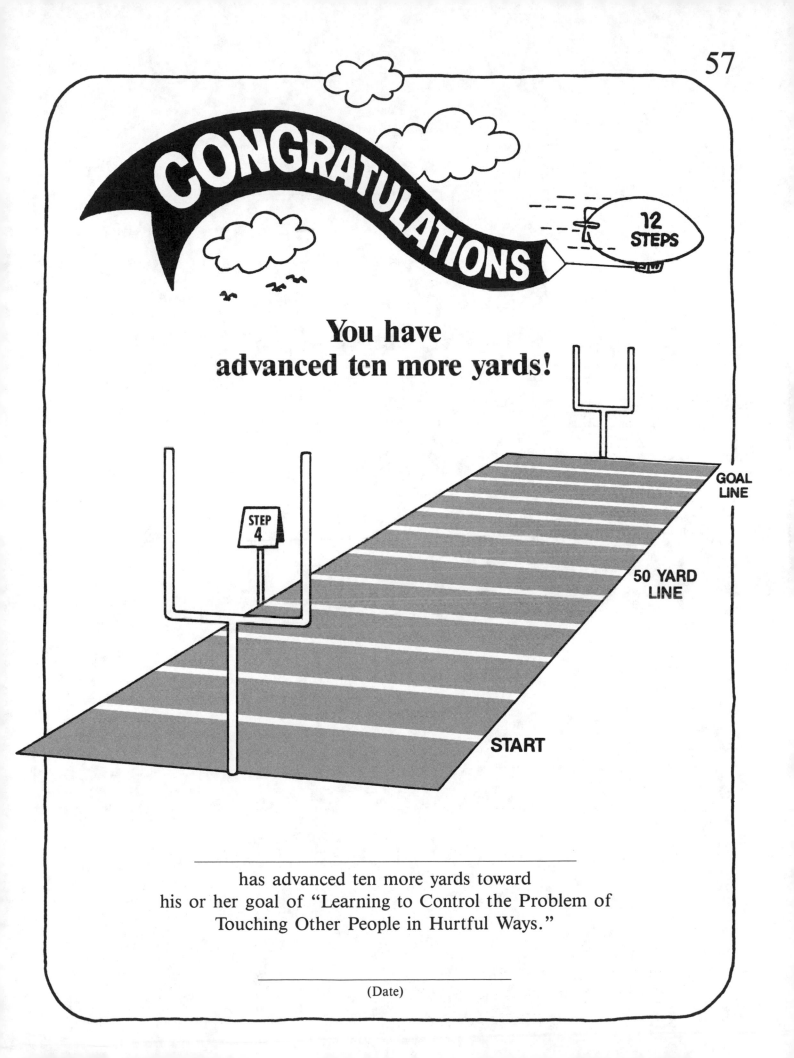

CONGRATULATIONS

**You have
advanced ten more yards!**

has advanced ten more yards toward
his or her goal of "Learning to Control the Problem of
Touching Other People in Hurtful Ways."

_____

(Date)

"I admit to myself, to other people, and to God, exactly what I have done that is wrong and harmful to others."

STEP

Read Step 5 to yourself (out loud) two times slowly.

"I admit to myself and to other people exactly what I have done that is wrong and harmful to others."

**ALTERNATE
STEP
5**

Read Step 5 to yourself (out loud) two times slowly.

WHAT WAS GOING ON INSIDE OF ME BEFORE I WAS HURTFUL

Now it's time to remember and write down what you said and what you thought about just *before* you touched someone else in a way that was wrong.

Before I Touched:

1. I was thinking... _____

_____

_____

2. I was feeling... _____

_____

_____

3. I said... _____

_____

_____

4. I was doing... _____

_____

_____

WHAT IS A VICTIM?

A victim is a person who is harmed by someone or something. A person who is a victim doesn't always show it and, sometimes, they don't even know it until later. Victims are people who have had something wrong or bad happen to them that wasn't their fault.

Put a check mark next to the reasons that go with what you did.

The person or people you touched are victims because of one or more of the following reasons:

1) _____ because they were younger or smaller than you.

2) _____ because they didn't want to be touched in that way.

3) _____ because you forced them or told them they had to do things they didn't want to do.

4) _____ because you tricked them into doing something.

5) _____ because they didn't know it was wrong.

6) _____ because they were too young or too scared to say no and run away.

7) _____ because you told them not to tell.

8) _____ because, even if they agreed to it, or started it, or acted like they liked it, they didn't know what would happen later or how they would feel afterwards.

9) _____ because you knew that it was wrong.

Can you think of any other reasons?

Do you understand why your victim is not being blamed for what happened?

Do you still feel like it was mostly his or her fault? Why?

Talk about those feelings.

If you were a victim of someone or something when you were younger, which of the nine reasons above made you a victim?

WHO I TOUCHED

It is important to remember, think about, and talk about the person or people whom you victimized, hurt, or touched in a way that was wrong. Close your eyes and picture that person or people in your mind. Then, fill in this page. (Use a separate page for each victim.)

The person whom I victimized is a: girl   boy   (circle one)

He/She was _____ years old when it happened.

I had known him/her for _____. (length of time)

His/Her name is _____.

Draw a picture of that person below:

Think about why you picked that person to victimize, and then talk about your reasons.

_____

_____

WHO I TOUCHED

It is important to remember, think about, and talk about the person or people whom you victimized, hurt, or touched in a way that was wrong. Close your eyes and picture that person or people in your mind. Then, fill in this page. (Use a separate page for each victim.)

The person whom I victimized is a: girl   boy   (circle one)

He/She was _____ years old when it happened.

I had known him/her for _____ . (length of time)

His/Her name is _____ .

Draw a picture of that person below:

Think about why you picked that person to victimize, and then talk about your reasons.

_____

_____

STEP 5
HOMEWORK
ASSIGNMENT
PART I

PUTTING YOURSELF IN SOMEONE ELSE'S SHOES

For one day next week, try to see what someone else's life is like by living for a while like they live or pretending to be them. This is called "putting yourself in someone else's shoes." For example, if you choose younger brothers or sisters, try eating what they eat, doing their chores, watching their favorite T.V. show, or helping them with their homework. You might choose someone who is very old — someone who walks and talks slowly and forgets things. You might choose someone who is handicapped. For example, someone who walks with a limp or a crutch or a cane; someone who is deaf (try cotton in your ears and write down everything you want to say on a pad of paper); or someone who is blind. If you decide to cover your eyes to try and see what being blind is like, always have someone walk beside you to make sure you don't hurt yourself.

_____   _____
(Parent Signature)   (Date)

WHAT IT IS THAT I DID

It is also important to remember *exactly* what you did to the other person or people. It is hard to think about things that you don't want to remember, but it is important to do if you are going to change.

What Happened

What I did:

1. First I did... _____

_____

_____

2. Then... _____

_____

_____

3. Then... _____

_____

_____

4. Then... _____

_____

_____

_____

What the other kid did:

1. First he/she... _____

_____

_____

2. Then... _____

_____

_____

3. Then... _____

_____

_____

4. Then... _____

_____

_____

_____

Part of remembering what you did is being able to picture it in your mind. You would probably rather block it out of your mind, but that won't make it go away. Picture what you did, in your mind, then draw it on this page. It's hard to do, but try.

If anything like this ever happened to you when you were younger, try to draw what that looked like. Tell somebody about it. Then talk about how it made you feel.

THOUGHTS AND FEELINGS DURING THE TOUCHING

Think back to when you were touching the other person. Where were you? Who else was there? Try to remember what you said and what you were thinking at the time. Think about what the other person said when you were doing the touching. How do you think he or she was feeling?

While I Was Touching

Me:

1. I said... _____

_____

_____

_____

2. I was thinking... _____

_____

_____

_____

3. I was feeling... _____

_____

_____

_____

The Other Kid:

1. He/She said... _____

_____

_____

_____

2. He/She might have been thinking...

_____

_____

_____

3. He/She probably was feeling... _____

_____

_____

_____

BEING AND DOING

Who you are and what you did are two different things. You are not a bad person just because you did a bad thing. Lots of good people sometimes do bad things. But they learn from their mistakes and they learn how to change their behavior. People who care about you don't like what you did but they still like *you*. It is important that *you* still like you, too.

In your last drawing, you drew a picture of what you did. On this page draw a picture of you.

See the difference between you and what you did? Which picture do you like better? Which one is the you that you want to be?

AFTER THE TOUCHING

Now that you've remembered and talked about the touching you did, think about what happened afterwards — how you were feeling, what you and the other kid said or did. Remember what you felt and thought *before* you got caught.

What Happened Afterward

Me:

1. I said . . . _____

_____

_____

2. What I did . . . _____

_____

_____

3. I thought about . . . _____

_____

_____

4. I was feeling . . . _____

_____

_____

The Other Kid:

1. He/She said . . . _____

_____

_____

2. What he/she did . . . _____

_____

_____

3. He/She might have thought . . . _____

_____

_____

4. He/She probably felt . . . _____

_____

_____

This has been the longest and hardest step of all. That's why you earn twice as many yards for this step than for any other step! You're learning that it takes a lot of hard work to control the problem of touching other people in hurtful ways. Being able to talk about your problem and your feelings is what this step is all about. How are you feeling now that you've finished this step? Write down or draw a picture of your feeling.

I am feeling _____

_____

STEP 5
HOMEWORK
ASSIGNMENT
PART II

ADMITTING MISTAKES

By the time most people grow up, they have made a few bad mistakes which they had to admit later. This week, find a grownup who made a mistake and admitted it. Ask him or her to tell you all about it. For example, what was the mistake? How did it happen? Whom was it admitted to? What made him or her admit it? How did he or she feel at the time? How does it feel now?

On this page, either you or the grownup should write down what the mistake was, and whom it was admitted to. Next week come back and describe it with the details. Try to remember the answers to all of the questions on this page.

The person who made the mistake was: _____

The mistake that he/she made was: _____

_____

_____

_____

The person or people it was admitted to were: _____

_____

_____   _____
(Parent Signature)   (Date)

76

The Step that I learned last week said (write down your answer or have someone else write it for you.)

_____

_____

_____

_____

_____

I practiced what I learned last week by _____

_____

_____

_____

_____

_____

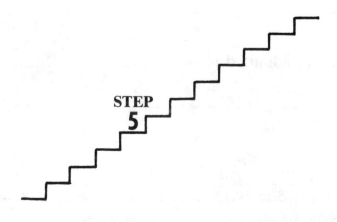

STEP
5

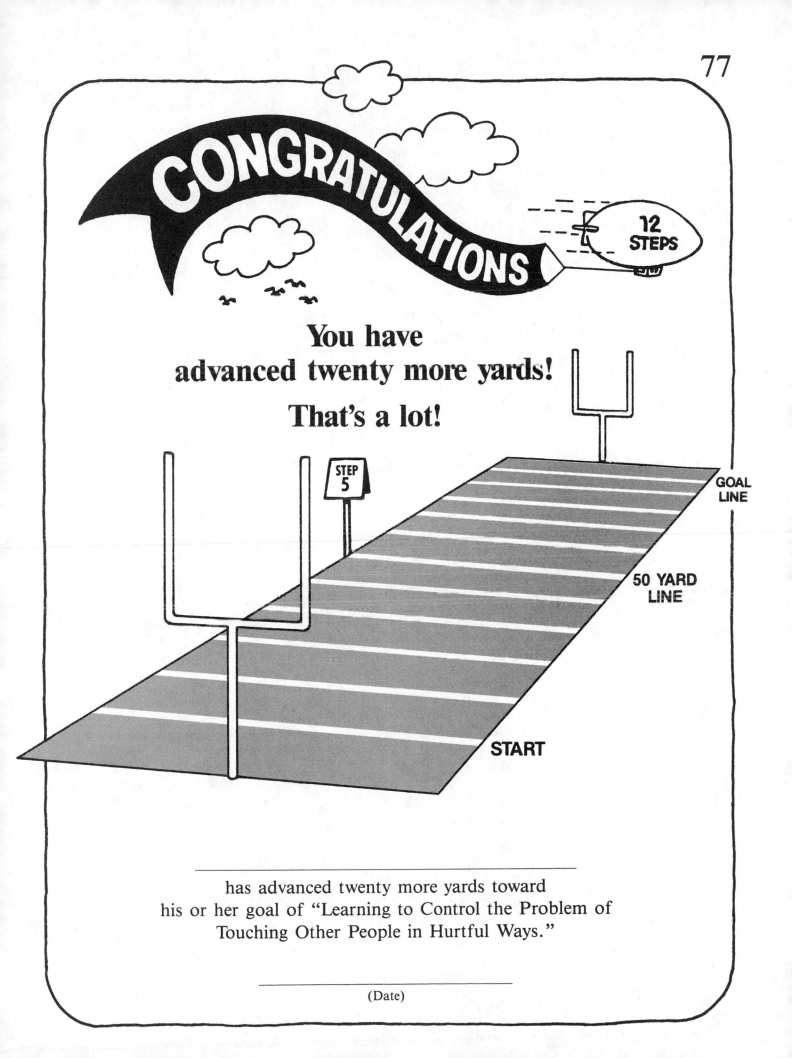

CONGRATULATIONS

12 STEPS

**You have
advanced twenty more yards!**

That's a lot!

STEP 5

GOAL LINE

50 YARD LINE

START

_____

has advanced twenty more yards toward
his or her goal of "Learning to Control the Problem of
Touching Other People in Hurtful Ways."

_____

(Date)

"I am ready to give up my problem (even though sometimes the touching feels good), and find another way to show my feelings."

STEP

6

Read Step 6 to yourself (out loud) two times slowly.

Draw a picture of you putting your problem along with the masks that you used to wear, into a balloon. Draw a picture of the balloon sailing off.

SELF-TALK

It is time to learn some new ways to deal with painful feelings —
ways that have nothing to do with touching. Along with talking to
other people about your feelings, you also can talk yourself into
feeling better. This is called "self-talk". It takes practice, but if you
get good at it, it can help you to handle scary or painful feelings.
These are some examples of self-talk that you can use:

"You have to have rain in order to get a rainbow."

"I'm mad, but I *can* control my anger."

"Everybody makes mistakes, I'll do better next time."

"Everybody is scared sometimes."

"It's okay to be sad, I have a good reason."

"I may not be perfect, but I'm special because I'm me."

"I might meet a new friend soon."

"Everyone has bad days — this is one of mine."

"Don't sweat the small stuff."

"I'll be okay tomorrow."

"There are lots of people who care about me."

"Chill out, cool it, hang in there."

Try making up some self-talk of your own. Practice
self-talk this week whenever you are feeling upset.

LETTING YOUR FEELINGS SHOW

What is the hardest feeling for you to express or show to other people? For example, is it hurt feelings, anger, fear, or some other feeling? What feeling do you most often stuff down inside of yourself? Think about it for a few minutes, then fill in the answer:

The feeling that is hardest for me to show is: _____

Think about what you usually do when you are feeling this way.
If you show this feeling at all, how do you show it to other people?

The way I act when I feel this way is: _____

_____

If you don't show this feeling very much or you act in a way that is different than you really feel, how do you know that you are feeling it? Think about the signs that tell you what you're feeling, then fill in the answer:

I know I'm feeling _____ because _____

_____

Now think about a way (or a better way) to show the feeling that is hardest for you to show. How could you show it so that other people can understand and help you with it?

I could show my _____ feeling by _____

_____

The next time you are feeling that way, try out your new way of showing it, on someone you know. Then come back and tell how it worked.

STEP 6
HOMEWORK
ASSIGNMENT

FEELINGS CHART

This week, keep track of the ways you let people know how you are feeling.

Feelings I had during the week:

1 _____

_____

_____

2 _____

_____

_____

3 _____

_____

_____

4 _____

_____

_____

The way that I let people know was:

1 _____

_____

_____

2 _____

_____

_____

3 _____

_____

_____

4 _____

_____

_____

_____   _____
(Parent Signature)   (Date)

84

The Step that I learned last week said (write down your answer or have someone else write it for you.)

_____

_____

_____

_____

_____

I practiced what I learned last week by _____

_____

_____

_____

_____

_____

_____

STEP
6

CONGRATULATIONS

12 STEPS

You have advanced ten more yards!

STEP 6

GOAL LINE

50 YARD LINE

START

YOU HAVE NOW COMPLETED 6 STEPS!

has advanced ten more yards toward
his or her goal of "Learning to Control the Problem of
Touching Other People in Hurtful Ways."

(Date)

"I am learning that there are some things about myself that I can change, and other things that I cannot change. I am working on changing the things I can."

STEP

7

Read Step 7 to yourself (out loud) two times slowly.

THINGS I WISH I COULD CHANGE

Each and every one of us has things about ourselves that we don't like and wish we could change. Those things usually have to do with the way we look (appearance), the way we act (behavior), the way we do things (performance), or the way we feel inside (emotions).

Make a list of the things about yourself that you don't like and want to change.

Things about my appearance that I wish I could change:

1 _____

2 _____

3 _____

4 _____

Things about my behavior that I wish I could change:

1 _____

2 _____

3 _____

4 _____

Things that I don't do very well that I wish I could change:

1 _____

2 _____

3 _____

4 _____

Feelings that I don't like having that I wish I could change:

1 _____

2 _____

3 _____

4 _____

THINGS
I CANNOT
CHANGE

There are some things about ourselves that we can change (like the way we act in certain situations), and some things about ourselves that we cannot change (like the color of our eyes, certain feelings, etc.).

Look carefully at the list you just made. What are the things on your list about yourself that you *can* change? What are the things on your list that you *cannot* change?

Put the things you can change about yourself on one side of the paper and the things you cannot change about yourself on the other side.

**Things on my list that
I CAN change:**

1 _____
_____
2 _____
_____
3 _____
_____
4 _____
_____
5 _____
_____

**Things on my list that
I CANNOT change:**

1 _____
_____
2 _____
_____
3 _____
_____
4 _____
_____
5 _____
_____

MY PLAN
FOR CHANGE

For each thing about yourself that you *can* change, make a plan and decide how and what you can do to make that change. You may need someone to help you make your plan. Who will it be?

These are things I CAN change about myself:

1 _____

2 _____

3 _____

This is how I am going to change:

1 _____

2 _____

3 _____

This person can help me:

1 _____

2 _____

3 _____

THE CRITIC
INSIDE YOU

Sometimes we spend a lot of time thinking about the things that we cannot change about ourselves. We have a voice inside ourselves that always reminds us about these things that we cannot change. Some people call this voice their "critic" because it criticizes us and puts us down. Some person's critic might say, "Your hair is ugly," or "You're dumb," or "You're not good enough." Do you have a name for the critical voice inside of you?

You can picture your critic as looking like a big vulture who stands over you saying negative things to you. What does your vulture say to you that makes you feel badly? Write some of those things inside the vulture's voice balloons.

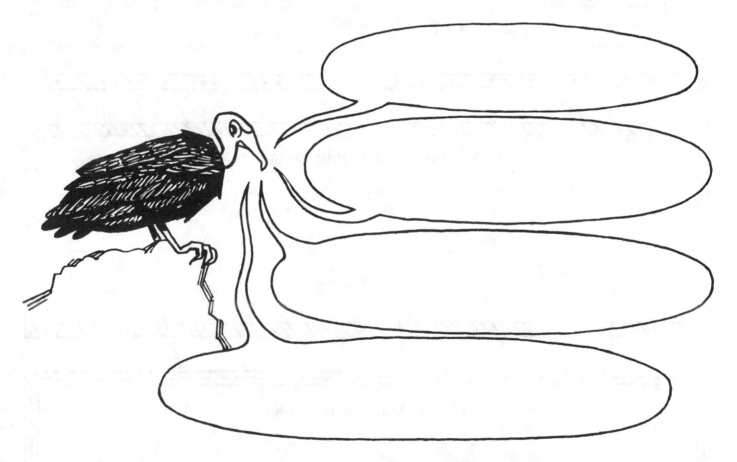

You need to learn to keep the vulture quiet by saying "Stop!" to that voice inside of you. You can answer it back by saying: "That's not true!" Remember, he's *your* vulture because he's really just *you* criticizing yourself. That's why he appears when you're feeling badly about yourself. You have created him; you can make him go away. Try stopping your vulture this week.

THINGS
I WOULDN'T
CHANGE

Now that you are learning to talk to the critical vulture who says negative things about you, let's look at the things about you that are special — the things you like about yourself. Make a list of the good things about you that you want to keep.

Things about my appearance that I like:

1 _____

2 _____

3 _____

4 _____

Turn the page for more...

Things that I do well are:

1 _____
2 _____
3 _____
4 _____

Good behaviors or feelings that I have are:

1 _____
2 _____
3 _____
4 _____

Nice things that other people say about me are:

1 _____
2 _____
3 _____
4 _____

STEP 7
HOMEWORK
ASSIGNMENT

CHANGING YOURSELF

Pick something you do that you would like to change. Pick something simple to start with — like forgetting to do your chores, daydreaming, or biting your nails. Make a plan for how to change that behavior. (Deciding to stop doing something is not enough. Figure out *how* you will stop and who will help you.) Ask someone to help you with your plan. Carry out your plan for one week. Then come back and tell how it went.

MY PLAN FOR CHANGE

The thing I do that I want to change is: _____

_____

The way I plan to change it is: _____

_____

_____

The people who will help me are: _____

_____

_____

_____   _____
(Parent Signature)   (Date)

The Step that I learned last week said (write down your answer or have someone else write it for you.)

_____

_____

_____

_____

_____

I practiced what I learned last week by _____

_____

_____

_____

_____

_____

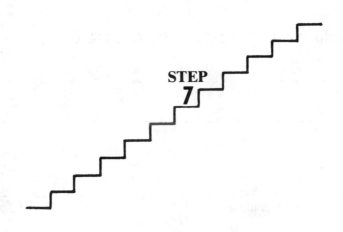

STEP
7

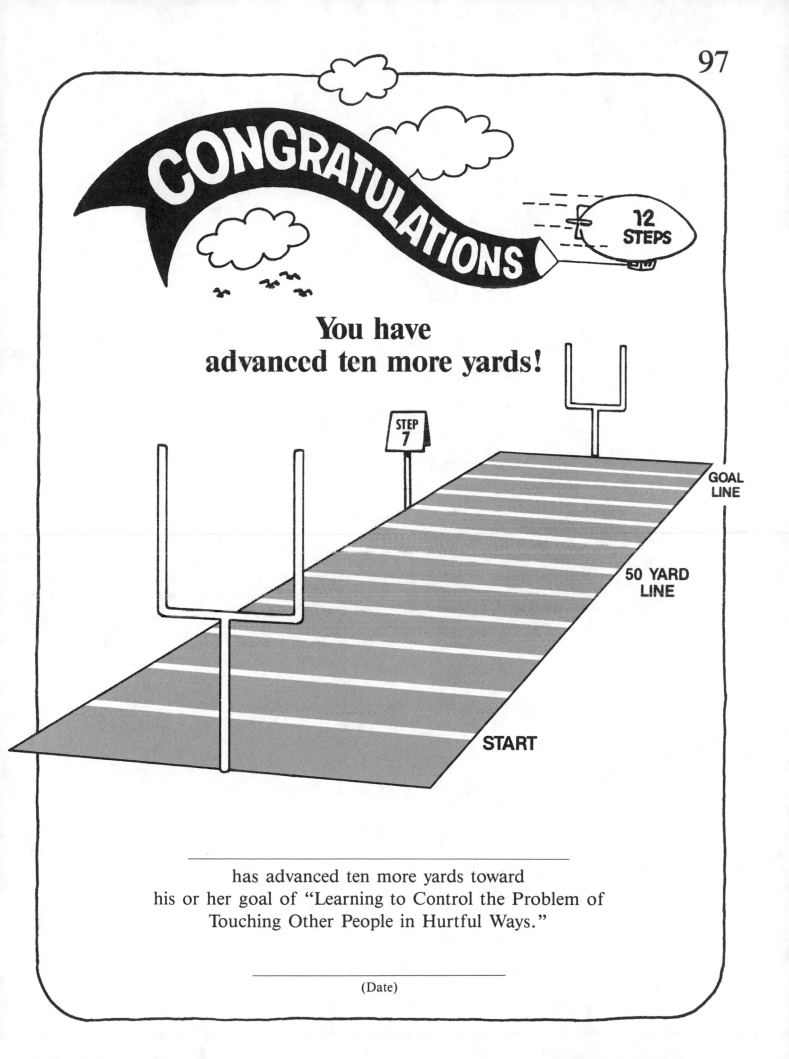

has advanced ten more yards toward
his or her goal of "Learning to Control the Problem of
Touching Other People in Hurtful Ways."

_____

(Date)

"I accept that I cannot change other people or their behavior. They are the only ones who can change themselves — and only if they want to. This includes my parents, other grownups, and my friends."

STEP

Read Step 8 to yourself (out loud) two times slowly.

THINGS
THAT BUG
ME

Make a list of the things about others
that really bug you.

Names of people:	Things that you would like them to change:
1 _____	1 _____
_____	_____
_____	_____
_____	_____
2 _____	2 _____
_____	_____
_____	_____
_____	_____
3 _____	3 _____
_____	_____
_____	_____
_____	_____
4 _____	4 _____
_____	_____

Remember, you cannot change other people. What things can you say to yourself to accept that you can't change others and that you are not responsible for them? Practice saying them out loud to yourself.

Now look at your list of things people do that really bug you. Make a list on this page of things that you could say to yourself about each of those "buggy" things. Remember, you can *ask* people to change but you can't *make* them change. You *can* help yourself feel less bugged.

1 _____

_____

_____

2 _____

_____

_____

3 _____

_____

_____

4 _____

_____

P.S. Many of the things that bug us the most are pretty small things. So, a good motto to remember is: Don't Sweat the Small Stuff!

STEP 8
HOMEWORK
ASSIGNMENT

Make a list of one thing that you like about each member of your family (including yourself), and one thing that you wish was different. Put a check mark next to the things you think you can change. Put a zero next to the things that only they can change. Show your list to your family, if you feel like it.

Person's Name	Something I Like About Them

STEP 8
HOMEWORK
ASSIGNMENT

Something I Wish Was Different	Who Can Change It

_____ _____
(Parent Signature)   (Date)

The Step that I learned last week said (write down your answer or have someone else write it for you.)

_____

_____

_____

_____

_____

I practiced what I learned last week by _____

_____

_____

_____

_____

_____

_____

STEP
8

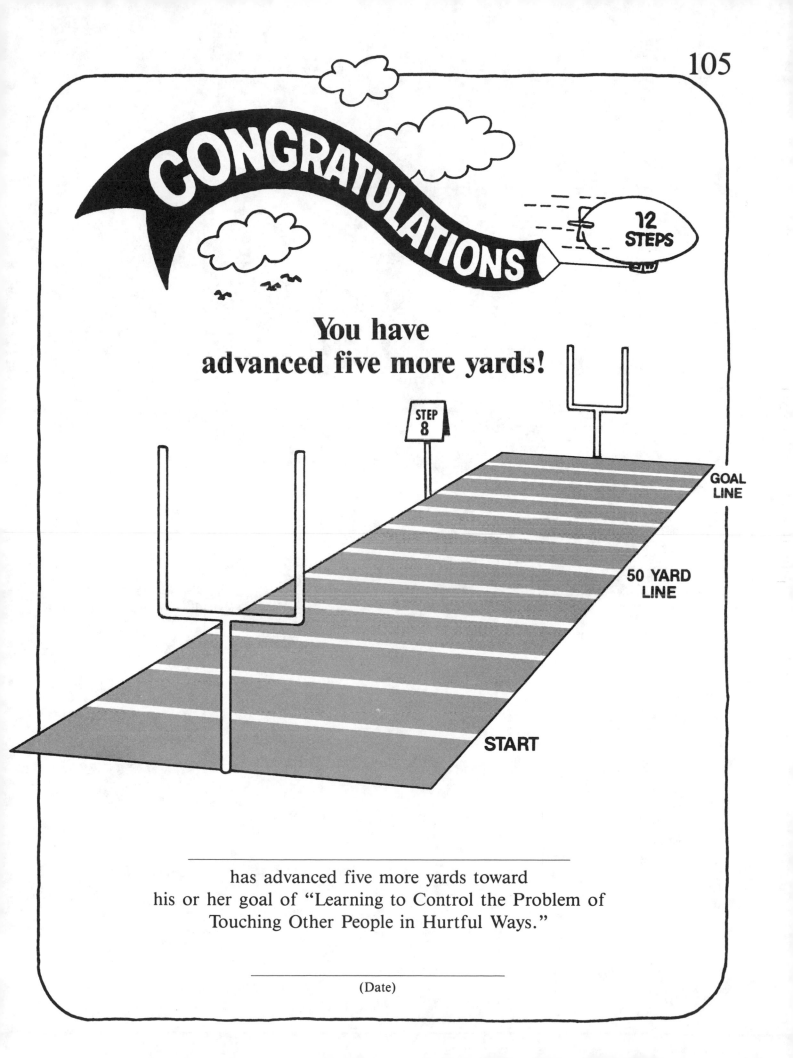

CONGRATULATIONS

12 STEPS

**You have
advanced five more yards!**

STEP 8

GOAL LINE

50 YARD LINE

START

_____

has advanced five more yards toward
his or her goal of "Learning to Control the Problem of
Touching Other People in Hurtful Ways."

_____

(Date)

"I am learning to recognize the times when I need help from others, including God, and I am willing to ask for help because I need it."

STEP

9

Read Step 9 to yourself (out loud) two times slowly.

"I am learning to recognize the times when I need help from others, and I am willing to ask for help because I need it."

ALTERNATE STEP

9

Read Step 9 to yourself (out loud) two times slowly.

Make a list or write a description of the different times lately that you've asked for help. Whom did you ask?

HELP!

Draw a picture of you asking for help.

Make a list of some things that you think you might need help with in the future.

1 _____

_____

_____

2 _____

_____

_____

3 _____

_____

_____

4 _____

_____

_____

_____

5 _____

_____

_____

6 _____

_____

MY
DANGER
SIGNS

Our bodies and our minds have ways of telling us when something is wrong or when we're feeling certain things. For example, getting goose bumps on your skin when you're cold, or a knot in your stomach when you're nervous, or having a nightmare after you've seen a scary movie, are all messages from your body or your mind that tell you how you're feeling. They are called "danger signs" because they warn you that there will be trouble ahead if don't pay attention to them and get help.

Think about the feeling, thinking, and body messages that will let you know that you might be in danger of touching someone again in ways that are wrong. Can you remember any danger signs, thoughts, or body messages that you had just before you touched someone the last time?

Now think about the *feelings* you might get that would make you want to touch someone again in a way that is wrong. Write down these feelings so that you will not forget them.

DANGER ZONE
BEWARE
CAUTION
TROUBLE AHEAD
WATCH OUT
DANGER
WAKE UP
HELP!
BE CAREFUL
WARNING

MY DANGER SIGN FEELINGS

_____

_____

_____

_____

(Remember, it's O.K. to have feelings. It's not O.K. to touch in hurtful ways just because you have certain feelings. You can do other things with your feelings.)

MY BODY MESSAGES

Sometimes our bodies give us messages or warning signs that tell us we're upset or that we may be heading for trouble. Think about the signs your body gives you when you're thinking about touching. Mark them on the drawing. Then talk about them.

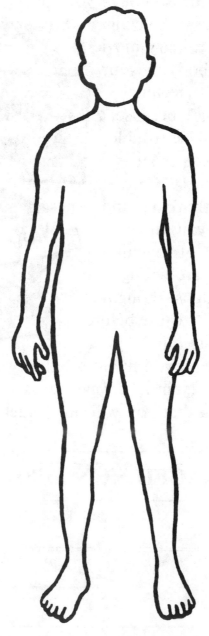

What can you do if your body gives you messages that it wants to touch or be touched in ways that are wrong? One thing you can do is physical exercise — like running or riding your bike. What else could you do? How about asking someone to help you control those body feelings? Whom will you ask?

DANGER SIGN THOUGHTS

There are times when you might start thinking about what you did or what you might do again if you have the chance. Picturing it in your mind might even get you turned on or excited. Those kinds of thoughts (which some people call "fantasies") are "Danger Sign" thoughts and they should tell you that you need to talk to someone and ask for help right away.

Danger Sign thoughts can lead to bad messages you say to yourself. Remember the vulture who criticizes you? This is like another vulture in your head who says negative things about your touching problem. Things like: "I don't care if I get in trouble or hurt someone else, I want to do it anyway." Write down some dangerous things that you or your vulture might say to you when you're having these kinds of thoughts.

VULTURE TALK

1. " _____ "

_____

2. " _____ "

_____

3. " _____ "

_____

You know how to talk back to that vulture. You learned it in Step #6. You can tell him to stop, you can tell him he's wrong, and you can make those bad thoughts and messages go away. Write down the things you will say to that vulture and to yourself that will help the Danger Sign thoughts disappear.

VULTURE BACK-TALK

1. " _____
_____
_____ "

2. " _____
_____
_____ "

3. " _____
_____
_____ "

4. " _____
_____
_____ "

DANGEROUS SITUATIONS

Certain situations also can be dangerous for kids who are trying to control their problem with touching. Situations are dangerous if they can make it harder for you to control your touching. Examples of situations that might be dangerous are: being left alone with the kid you touched or with someone who reminds you of that kid; being alone when you're angry or upset; or hanging around with older kids who get into trouble or talk a lot about sex.

What kinds of situations do you think could be dangerous for you these days? (Hint: If you say "none", then you have forgotten that your problem is bigger than you are.)

Draw or write down some of the situations that might make it hard for you to control your touching. Use the next page if you need more space to draw.

How can you avoid being in these situations? Whom will you ask to help you?

118

DANGEROUS SITUATIONS

STEP 9
HOMEWORK
ASSIGNMENT

During the week, pay attention to when you are upset and find yourself reacting strongly to something, when things are going wrong, when you're getting mad or somebody's mad at you, or when you're really scared or crying or getting into a fight. When it's all over and you're feeling better, sit down and answer these questions:

1. What happened just before you got upset? _____

_____

_____

2. What were your feelings when you started to react? _____

_____

3. Where did you feel it in your body? _____

_____

4. What other signals told you how strongly you were feeling? _____

_____

_____

5. What did you do to calm yourself down afterward? _____

_____

6. How do you feel about it now? _____

_____

_____   _____
(Parent Signature)   (Date)

120

The Step that I learned last week said (write down your answer or have someone else write it for you.)

_____

_____

_____

_____

_____

I practiced what I learned last week by _____

_____

_____

_____

_____

_____

_____

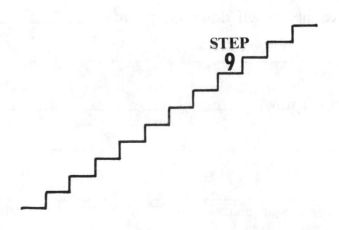
STEP
9

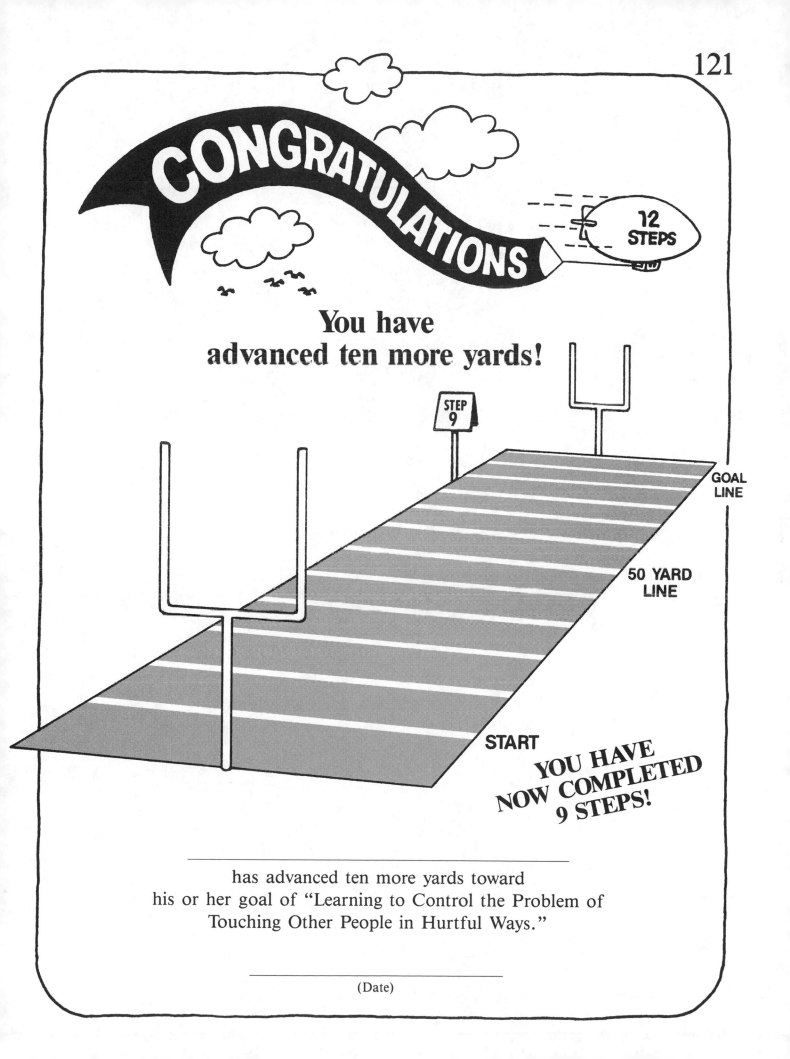

CONGRATULATIONS

12 STEPS

You have
advanced ten more yards!

STEP 9

GOAL LINE

50 YARD LINE

START

YOU HAVE NOW COMPLETED 9 STEPS!

_____

has advanced ten more yards toward
his or her goal of "Learning to Control the Problem of
Touching Other People in Hurtful Ways."

_____

(Date)

"I have made a list of everyone whom I have hurt by my behavior (including myself), and I will try to make up, in any way I can, for the harm that I have caused."

STEP
10

Read Step 10 to yourself (out loud) two times slowly.

MY AMENDS LIST

Think about all of the people that you've hurt with your touching problem. Make a list of the people that you've hurt, and try to think of a way to make up for the hurt. Some people call this "making amends".

Who I've hurt:

1 _____   4 _____

2 _____   5 _____

3 _____   6 _____

How I've hurt them:

1 _____   4 _____

2 _____   5 _____

3 _____   6 _____

How I'd like to make up for the hurt:

1 _____   4 _____

2 _____   5 _____

3 _____   6 _____

It is not always possible to make up for what you did, to some people. It may not be possible to have any contact with them. When that is the situation, what kinds of things could you do instead?

Maybe you could prepare yourself to do something in case you ever get the chance, when you're older. Maybe you can do something for someone else, instead. Maybe you can work very hard on controlling your problem so that you won't have to make amends to anyone else.

What else could you do? Draw or write it here.

STEP 10
HOMEWORK
ASSIGNMENT

Remember a time when you did something mean to someone else, or something dishonest like lying or stealing, or when you hurt somebody's feelings (even if you didn't mean to do it). It doesn't matter how long ago it was or whether they still remember it. Now, figure out a way to "make amends" to that person and do it this week. For example, you could go and tell them you're sorry for what you did or you could write them a letter. If they don't remember what happened, you should remind them of what you know you did, even if they didn't know about it.

STEP 10
HOMEWORK
ASSIGNMENT

MY AMEND

1. What I did that I needed to apologize for: _____

_____

_____

_____

2. Whom I made my amend to: _____

3. What I did or said: _____

_____

_____

_____

4. How I was feeling when I made my amend: _____

_____

_____

5. The way I feel now that it's over: _____

_____

_____

_____   _____

(Parent Signature)   (Date)

128

The Step that I learned last week said (write down your answer or have someone else write it for you.)

_____

_____

_____

_____

_____

I practiced what I learned last week by _____

_____

_____

_____

_____

_____

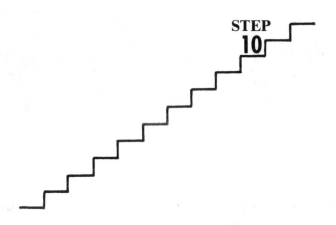

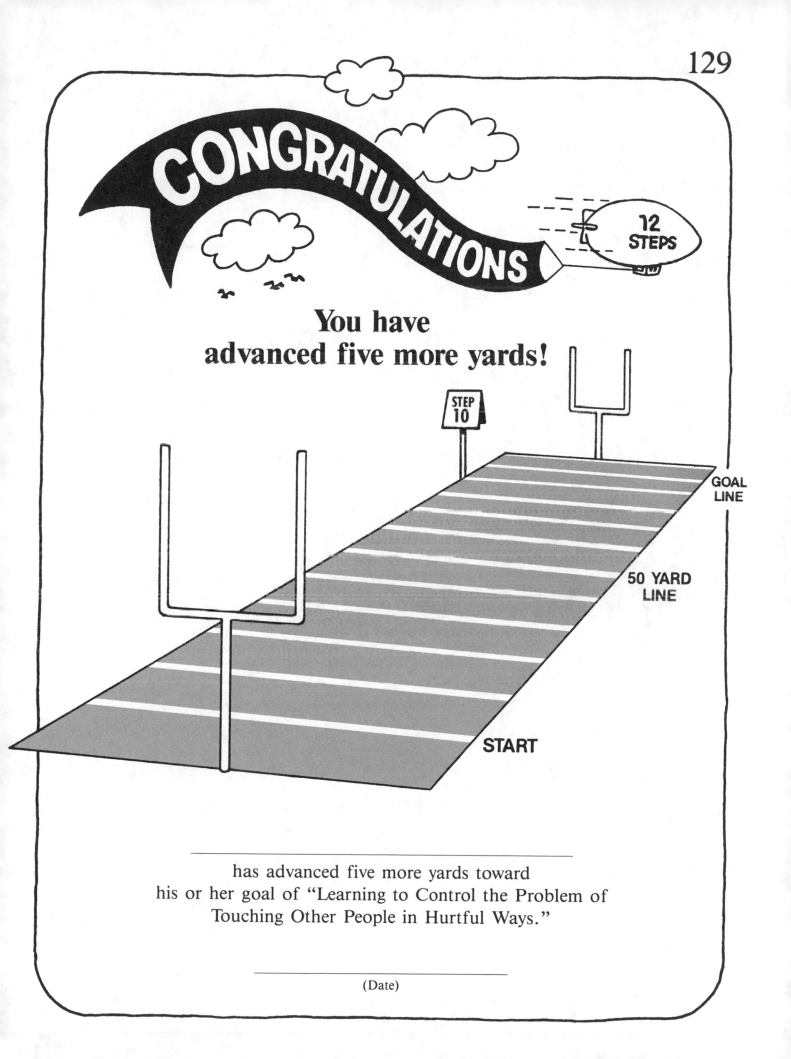

has advanced five more yards toward
his or her goal of "Learning to Control the Problem of
Touching Other People in Hurtful Ways."

(Date)

"I continue to think about my problem and I am willing to ask for help if I feel it coming back."

STEP
11

Read Step 11 to yourself (out loud) two times slowly.

MY DANGER SIGNS

It is very important to remember your danger signs. Write them or draw them on this page.

My danger signs:

Thinking...

Feeling...

Doing...

Situations...

How I will ask for help:

When you feel your danger signs coming back, what things will you do?
Write them here.

DANGER

1 _____

_____

_____

2 _____

_____

_____

3 _____

_____

_____

4 _____

_____

_____

5 _____

_____

_____

STEP 11
HOMEWORK
ASSIGNMENT

Take time to stop and think about your touching problem at least once this week. Think about all the things you've said and heard about it as you have worked through the steps. Write down what you are thinking or saying to yourself about your problem now. Here are some sentences to fill in, to get you started.

1. I still think that my touching problem is _____

_____

2. When I think about my problem I feel _____

_____

3. I think I did it because _____

_____

4. I think therapy is _____

_____

5. I think I am _____

_____

6. Other thoughts I have about my problem: _____

_____

_____

_____

STEP 11
HOMEWORK
ASSIGNMENT

Now write down at least three things you have learned about your problem since you started therapy.

1 _____

_____

_____

_____

2 _____

_____

_____

_____

3 _____

_____

_____

_____

_____   _____
(Parent Signature)   (Date)

136

The Step that I learned last week said (write down your answer or have someone else write it for you.)

_____

_____

_____

_____

_____

I practiced what I learned last week by _____

_____

_____

_____

_____

_____

_____

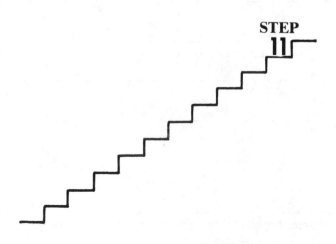

STEP
11

has advanced five more yards, and has just about reached his or her goal of "Learning to Control the Problem of Touching Other People in Hurtful Ways."

_____

(Date)

"I will help other kids who have this problem by sharing my own problem and feelings, and by helping them to see that it is too tough to handle by themselves."

STEP 12

Read Step 12 to yourself (out loud) two times slowly.

Make a list of the ways you might be able to help other kids who have this touching problem.

1 _____

_____

_____

2 _____

_____

_____

3 _____

_____

_____

4 _____

_____

_____

How will you know that they have a problem?

_____

_____

_____

_____

_____

Draw yourself sharing and helping other kids with the same problem.

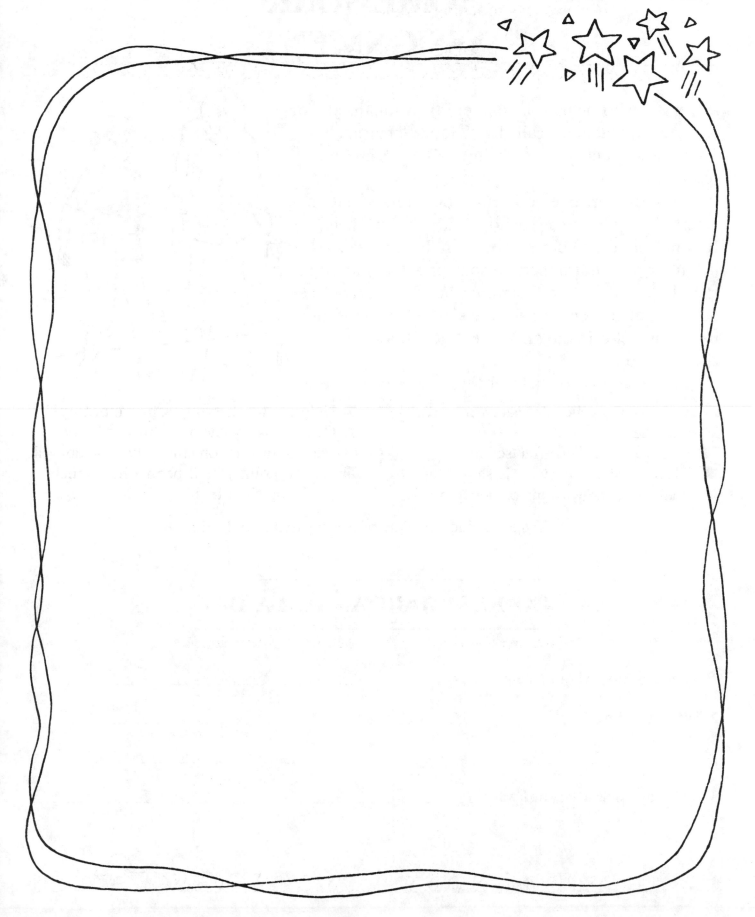

STEP 12
HOMEWORK
ASSIGNMENT

A person who helps someone else just for the joy of helping is sometimes called a "Good Samaritan". Your assignment is to try being a Good Samaritan for a day.

Think of someone you know, or find a situation where there is someone who could use your help. It could be a member of your family, a friend, a neighbor, a handicapped person, or a kid you don't even know. Think of something helpful you could do for that person and then ask if he or she would like your help. If the answer is "no", find someone else to help.

Some examples of helpful things you might do are:

- Help your brother or sister (or parents) with their chores
- Help your teacher after school
- Cheer someone up who is sad or upset
- Help someone with his or her homework

- Help to stop a fight from happening
- Call or visit someone who is sick
- Teach someone something that you do well
- (Bonus points): Tell people how much you appreciate them.

What are some other helpful things you could do?

GOOD SAMARITAN FOR A DAY

1. The person(s) whom I helped was _____

2. What I did was _____

_____

3. The way I felt afterward was _____

_____ _____
(Parent Signature)   (Date)

The Step that I learned last week said (write down your answer or have someone else write it for you.)

_____

_____

_____

_____

_____

I practiced what I learned last week by _____

_____

_____

_____

_____

_____

_____

STEP
12

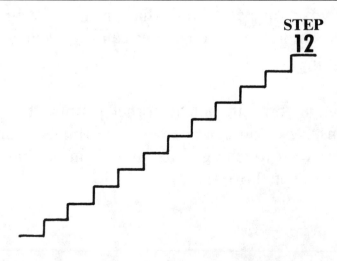

LESSONS
LEARNED

If you have completed all the steps, you have worked hard on your problem with touching. The twelve steps are here to help you learn about yourself and your problem. Here are a few of the things we hope you learned.

Put a ✔ next to the things you know you have learned about yourself.

Put a ✗ next to the things you're not so sure about.

1 ____ Your problem is too tough for you to handle by yourself — but it's not too tough to handle if you get help. You *can* control what you do, and other people can help.

2 ____ You know how to ask for help, and you know who the people are who will help you. All you need to do is ask.

3 ____ You can help yourself, too. You can show your honest feelings to people who can help you handle them — especially when you are upset. You also can use self-talk to make yourself feel better. You even know how to talk back to your "vulture voice" when he gives you negative messages that could get you in trouble.

4 ____ Everybody makes mistakes sometimes — including you. You don't need to blame other people for things that are really your fault. You can admit when you do something wrong. You can even learn important lessons from your mistakes.

5 ____ You can change yourself, but not other people. It is their problem to change themselves. You can change some things about yourself — especially your problem with touching — but you cannot change other things. You can learn to accept those things.

6 ____ Good people sometimes do bad things. You are not a bad person just because you do some things that are wrong. The people who love you still love you, even if they hate what you did. You can still love yourself, too.

7 ____ You are learning to think about other people's feelings and how to put yourself in someone else's shoes. You know that what you did wasn't wrong just because you got into trouble — it's wrong because it could be hurtful to other people and because you didn't think about their feelings or how it could affect them.

8 ____ You know that your body and your mind have danger signs that can tell you when something is wrong or when you're feeling certain things. You know you should pay attention to them so that you can ask for help *before* you do something wrong.

9 ____ Your problem is not gone just because you understand it better. You need to stay on the lookout for it and for the feelings that go with it, so that you're ready to stop them. If you start to think that you are safe and that you do not have a problem anymore, that's when it could sneak up on you.

10 ____ You know the difference between good touching and bad touching for kids, and you know that you still have to be careful about whom you touch and how you touch. You can control your urge to touch in ways that are wrong, but you can still enjoy good touching. You can do that because you want to and because you know that there are lots of people who will help you. They know that you are a special person.

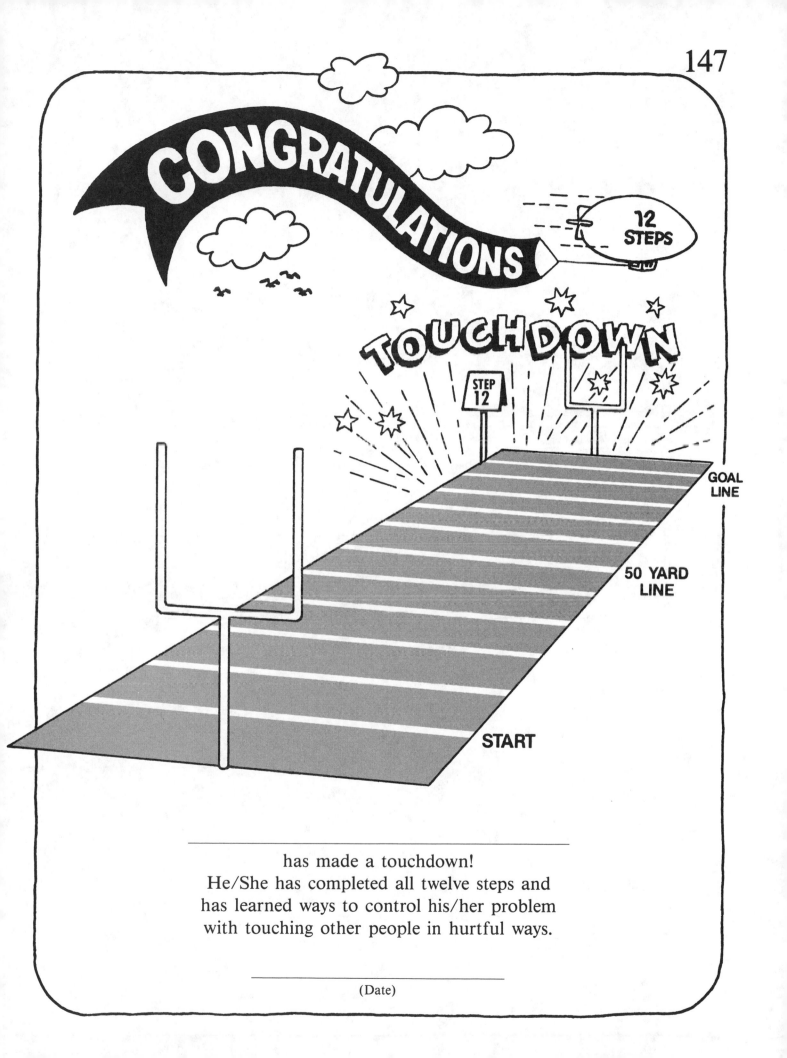

_____

has made a touchdown!
He/She has completed all twelve steps and
has learned ways to control his/her problem
with touching other people in hurtful ways.

_____

(Date)

HAPPY HEALTH

You've made it through the twelve steps. Be proud of yourself! You are on the road to recovery. You are becoming stronger and healthier day by day. Draw a picture of something happy on this last page and ask for a hug from the person or people who helped you complete this workbook.

EXTRA DRAWING PAGE

EXTRA DRAWING PAGE

AUTHORS' BIOGRAPHICAL INFORMATION

Kee MacFarlane is the director of the Child Sexual Abuse Center and founder of the Support Program for Abuse-Reactive Kids (SPARK) at Children's Institute International in Los Angeles, California. She is a social worker and nationally recognized expert in the field of child sexual abuse. She has received numerous awards during her seventeen years in the field of child abuse for her work on behalf of victims, perpetrators, and families. She serves as a consultant, trainer, and board member to dozens of state and national organizations involved with the social, legal, and clinical aspects of child maltreatment. She is the author of more than forty chapters, articles, and publications in the area of child abuse; she is the editor of *Child Sexual Abuse: Selected Readings;* and a co-author of the book, *Sexual Abuse of Young Children,* published by Guilford Press. She is married and the mother of two young stepchildren.

Carolyn Cunningham is the executive director of the Children's Center of the Antelope Valley, a comprehensive child abuse center. She is the former director of the Young Offenders Program at Glendale Family Services in Los Angeles.

Formerly an elementary school teacher, she is a licensed marriage, family, and child counselor who has worked with children and families for fifteen years, including seven years in the area of child sexual abuse treatment. She is on the advisory board of the National Adolescent Perpetrators Network, and is on the board of directors for the National Council for Sexual Addiction. She is the author of *The Separation Book,* a workbook for young children who have experienced separation or loss, also published by KIDSRIGHTS.

KIDSRIGHTS
Professional Videos

☐ KIDS IN COURT

Designed to provide children and their parents with an audio visual teaching aid about court proceedings and testimony. Reduces the anxiety a child experiences when participating in this complex system. A must for social workers, attorneys, vicitms' assistants. Covers: Reasons for Going to Court; The Courthouse; The Hearing or Trial; Post Trial/Hearing Letdown. Comes with a comprehensive book.

#4635-V Video, 20 min., All Ages   **$195.00**

☐ SUFFERING IN SILENCE:
Sexual Assault Survivors

Expertly presented scenarios are based upon actual cases, each recounting their history of abuse as children; the impact upon them; and detailing their steps to recovery. Provides a catharsis for support groups.

#4620-V Video, 22 min., Prof.   **$225.00**

☐ CHILD'S ACCOUNT: *The use of anatomically correct dolls in the investigation of child sexual abuse*

Designed for child welfare workers, supervisors, psychologists. The information in this video will also be of use to police, physicians, and any professional who comes in contact with abused children. This program assumes no prior experience in the use of anatomically correct dolls, and reassures that one need not be an 'expert' to use anatomical dolls effectively. Includes a detailed facilitator's manual.

#4630-V Video, 24 min., Prof.   **$195.00**
#4839 Additional Manuals each   **$7.50**

☐ CHILD ABUSE:
An Investigative Interview

Created by attorneys, police officers, social workers, and victim witness advocates. Presents dramatizations of proper and improper interviewing techniques. Shows concrete examples of how to conduct an interview which is legally sound and causes the least amount of emotional harm to a young child. Workbook highlights and supplements the material in the video.

For use by trainers of law enforcement and human service professionals who intervene at disclosure with sexually abused children.

#4634-V Video, 50 min., Prof.   **$195.00**

☐ LITTLE BEAR PROGRAM

This nationally recognized program for children age 4 to 9, uses animal characters to teach children ways to avoid being sexually abused. Accompanied by a 30 minute inservice video program for teachers and facilitators.

#4617-V Video, 30 min., Age 4-9   **$149.00**

☐ LITTLE BEAR TEACHER/LEADER
TRAINING VIDEO AND GUIDE

Following the actual Little Bear presentation, the teacher video emphasizes the need for both disclosure and abuse prevention methods. **The Little Bear Training Guide,** a comprehensive 24 page manual, accompanies the video. Suggested audiences: Teachers, counselors, and other leaders who work with sexual abuse prevention.

#4618-V Video, 30 min., Prof.   **$149.00**

#4619-V Both Videos–Special Price   **$249.00**

KIDSRIGHTS, 10100 PARK CEDAR DRIVE, CHARLOTTE, NC 28210 1-800/892-KIDS OR 704/541-0100 FAX: 704/541-0113

Please send me the materials I have checked above. I have added 8% for shipping and handling. Authorized purchase orders are accepted. Orders under $50 __must__ be prepaid. VISA/MasterCard payment welcome.

KIDSRIGHTS *most popular titles*
"Must Have" therapeutic tools
for professionals

☐ STEPS TO HEALTHY TOUCHING

STEPS TO HEALTHY TOUCHING focuses on the problems and treatment of youngsters who themselves have been sexually abused and in turn victimize other children. This 150 page, 8 1/2" x 11" workbook combines a specialized interpretation of the Twelve Steps and Twelve Traditions along with interactive activities for the child, therapists discussions, and homework assignments that must be completed by the child and signed, providing a fully integrated treatment program. Provides a broad framework to support children in the life-transforming move from self-defeating behavior to healthy coping. By Kee MacFarlane & Carolyn Cunningham.

#4423 Paper, 150p., 8 1/2" x 11", ages 5-12   1-4 **$19.95 each**
Order in quantity and Save!   5+ **$17.95 each**   25+ **$14.95 each**

☐ THE OPPOSITIONAL CHILD

How to recognize and change the self-defeating behavior of a child (or adult) who persists in doing the opposite of what he should do, and the opposite of what he really wants to do. Straightforward, insightful. Recommended. By O. Randall Braman, Ph.D.

#4807 Paper, 121p.   **$9.95**

☐ COMMON SOLUTIONS FOR THE UNCOMMON CHILD

A unique presentation; gives teachers quick, effective strategies for dealing with the learning disabled or behavior disordered student in their class. Twenty-five profiles, including entertaining drawings, provide characteristic behaviors. The strategy section in the back of the book provides the answers.

#4523 Paper, 120p., 8 1/2" x 11"   **$15.95**

☐ IT'S NOT YOUR FAULT

This book has two important purposes: to teach children who have been sexually molested that they were not responsible for the abuse, and, to teach all children basic sexual molestation prevention skills. Read-aloud sections and discussion questions. Fully illustrated.

#4325 Paper, 25p., Age 4-11 & Adult   **$3.95**
50+ **$3.55 each**   100+ **$3.15**

☐ CHILD SUPPORT:

through small group counseling
Recommended by counselors throughout the nation. Easily develop small group counseling sessions for ages 6 to 12. Issues include: Children of Alcoholics, Children of Incarcerated Parents, Children of Divorce, Peer Relations Groups, more.

#4520 Paper, 243p., 8 1/2" x 11"   **$24.95**

☐ BREAKAWAY NEW

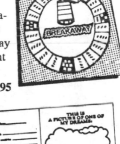

An educational game to inform adolescents about abuse and neglect and to explore nonaggressive responses to anger and frustration. Successfully used with 12-16 year olds and exceptional ed students. Also, a great way to educate & train new parents in non-violent discipline techniques.

#4480 Breakaway, 2-6 Players   **$39.95**

☐ ABOUT ME

This unique diagnostic tool clearly identifies a child's problem areas, and aids in identifying and expressing feelings. Pages opposite interactive questions are designed for self-expression. ABOUT ME can be used all at one time, or use one section for each visit. Each page is dated and includes a face-graph the child can check to determine how he or she feels. Sections include: Family, School, Feelings, and more. Large drawing area.

#4421 Workbook, 26p., 8 1/2" x 11", Age 3-13   1-9 **$3.95 each**
10+ **$3.55**   100+ **$2.55**   500+ **$2.55**   1,000+ **$1.95**   2,500+ **$1.65 each**

☐ ALL KINDS OF SEPARATION

An interactive workbook that clearly deals with a young child's feelings of abandonment and self-blame associated with a parental separation. Scenarios include: drug and alcohol abuse, sexual or physical abuse, divorce, hospitalization. Evocative illustrations and therapeutic text introduce skills a child can use to work through these feelings.

#4422 Workbook, 24p., 8 1/2" x 11", Age 3-13   1-9 **$3.95 each**
10+ **$3.55**   100+ **$3.15**   500+ **$2.55**   1,000+ **$1.95**   2,500+ **1.65 each**

KIDSRIGHTS, 10100 PARK CEDAR DRIVE, CHARLOTTE, NC 28210 1-800/892-KIDS OR 704/541-0100 FAX: 704/541-0113
Please send me the materials I have checked above. I have added 8% for shipping and handling. Authorized purchase orders are accepted. Orders under $50 must be prepaid. VISA/MasterCard payment welcome.

NOTES:

NOTES:

NOTES: